C-1892

MW00483834

THIS IS YOUR **PASSBOOK**® FOR ...

ACTUARIAL PROBABILITY EXAM (P)

NATIONAL LEARNING CORPORATION®
passbooks.com

PASSBOOK® SERIES

THE *PASSBOOK® SERIES* has been created to prepare applicants and candidates for the ultimate academic battlefield – the examination room.

At some time in our lives, each and every one of us may be required to take an examination – for validation, matriculation, admission, qualification, registration, certification, or licensure.

Based on the assumption that every applicant or candidate has met the basic formal educational standards, has taken the required number of courses, and read the necessary texts, the *PASSBOOK® SERIES* furnishes the one special preparation which may assure passing with confidence, instead of failing with insecurity. Examination questions – together with answers – are furnished as the basic vehicle for study so that the mysteries of the examination and its compounding difficulties may be eliminated or diminished by a sure method.

This book is meant to help you pass your examination provided that you qualify and are serious in your objective.

The entire field is reviewed through the huge store of content information which is succinctly presented through a provocative and challenging approach – the question-and-answer method.

A climate of success is established by furnishing the correct answers at the end of each test.

You soon learn to recognize types of questions, forms of questions, and patterns of questioning. You may even begin to anticipate expected outcomes.

You perceive that many questions are repeated or adapted so that you can gain acute insights, which may enable you to score many sure points.

You learn how to confront new questions, or types of questions, and to attack them confidently and work out the correct answers.

You note objectives and emphases, and recognize pitfalls and dangers, so that you may make positive educational adjustments.

Moreover, you are kept fully informed in relation to new concepts, methods, practices, and directions in the field.

You discover that you arre actually taking the examination all the time: you are preparing for the examination by "taking" an examination, not by reading extraneous and/or supererogatory textbooks.

In short, this PASSBOOK®, used directedly, should be an important factor in helping you to pass your test.

ACTUARY

NATURE OF WORK

Actuaries are responsible for developing and keeping insurance and pension plans on a sound financial basis. Using mathematical methods and techniques, they develop and analyze statistical tables to evaluate the probability of loss on whatever is to be insured. They are concerned with mortality (death) and morbidity (sickness) rates, the frequency of injuries, and personal and property losses from fire, burglary, explosion, and other hazards. Taking into consideration the estimates of payments to policyholders, as well as estimates of their company's future expenses and investment income, actuaries determine the premium rates for each particular type of insurance policy. They also analyze company earnings and prepare policy contract provisions.

To perform their duties effectively, actuaries must keep abreast of general economic trends and legislative, health, social, and other developments that may affect the soundness of insurance practices. Because of their broad knowledge of the insurance field, actuaries frequently work on problems arising in several different departments of their companies, such as investment, underwriting, group insurance, and pension sales and service departments. Those in executive positions may help to determine general company policy and may testify before public agencies on proposed legislation which would affect the insurance business or on the justification for intended changes in company premium rates or contract provisions.

Actuaries employed by the Federal Government usually deal with a particular Government insurance or pension program, such as social security (old-age, survivors, disability, and health insurance) or life insurance for veterans and members of the Armed Forces. Actuaries in State government positions are involved in the supervision and regulation of insurance companies, in the operation of State retirement or pension systems, and they may work on problems connected with unemployment insurance or workmen's compensation. Consulting actuaries perform services, on a fee basis, for private companies, unions, and government agencies. They often set up employee pension and welfare plans and periodically make actuarial valuations of them.

WHERE EMPLOYED

Private insurance companies employ about two-thirds of all actuaries. Nearly nine-tenths of this group work for life insurance companies and the remainder work for property and casualty companies. The size of an insurance company's actuarial staff depends primarily upon the volume of its insurance work. Large companies may employ as many as 50 to 100 actuaries, whereas small companies may have only 1 or 2 actuaries on their staffs or may rely entirely on consulting firms or rating bureaus (associations which supply actuarial data to member companies).

Several hundred actuaries are employed by consulting firms or are in business for themselves. Significant numbers are also employed by private firms other than insurance companies to administer private pension and welfare plans. Others work for Federal and State Governments. Some are employed by property and casualty rating bureaus and a few teach in colleges and universities.

TRAINING, OTHER QUALIFICATIONS, AND ADVANCEMENT

A bachelor's degree with a major in mathematics is usually required for entry into actuarial work. Some new graduates with a major in such fields as economics or business administration and a minor in mathematics can qualify for beginning actuarial positions. Although only a few colleges and universities offer training specifically designed for actuarial careers, several hundred institutions offer the necessary courses. The mathematics courses that should be taken by the prospective actuary include algebra, analytical geometry, differential and integral calculus, mathematical statistics, and probability. Other desirable courses include insurance law, economics, investments, accounting and other aspects of business administration, and English composition and speech.

To gain full professional status, actuaries usually must pass a series of examinations, which cover general mathematics, specialized actuarial mathematics, and all phases of the insurance business. It is desirable for the student considering an actuarial career to take the beginning examinations covering general mathematics while he is still in college. Success in passing these examinations helps the student determine whether he has the ability to become an actuary. Also, those who pass have better opportunities for employment and a higher starting salary. The more advanced examinations, usually taken by those in junior actuarial positions, require extensive from study and experience in insurance work. It usually takes from 5 to 10 years after entering a beginning actuarial position to complete an entire series.

The actuarial examinations for the life insurance field are given by the Society of Actuaries, and those in property and casualty insurance by the Casualty Actuarial Society. Associate membership is awarded after completion of part of the examination series. The designation of "Fellow" is conferred after successful completion of either all 10 examinations given by the Society of Actuaries or the 8 examinations of the Casualty Actuarial Society.

Besides mathematical ability, applicants for beginning actuarial positions are likely to be evaluated also on personal characteristics, such as ability to deal with people, leadership qualities, and interest in business problems. Preference is given to applicants who have passed at least one or more of the actuarial examinations and who have experience provided in some insurance companies which hire and train college undergraduates during the summer months, for example.

A beginning actuary in an insurance company is usually rotated among different jobs in his department to learn the various actuarial operations and become familiar with the different phases of insurance work. At first, the trainee may make calculations or tabulations for actuarial tables or for the annual statement. Later, he may supervise actuarial clerks and prepare correspondence and reports.

Advancement to more responsible work as an assistant actuary and later as associate or chief actuary depends largely upon on-the-job performance and the number of actuarial examinations successfully completed. Some actuaries, because of their broad knowledge of the insurance and related fields, qualify for administrative positions in other company activities, particularly in the underwriting, accounting, or data-processing departments. A significant number of actuaries advance to top executive positions.

EMPLOYMENT OUTLOOK

Employment opportunities for actuaries are expected to be very good through this decade. New graduates who have the necessary mathematical education and who have passed some examinations of either professional society will be in particular demand.

Employment of actuaries is expected to increase in both the life and casualty insurance fields, primarily because of anticipated growth in the number and type of insurance policies and employee-benefit plans. More actuaries will be needed to solve the increasing number of problems arising from continuously changing and increasingly complex insurance and pension coverage. The rapidly growing number of group life insurance plans and health and pension plans will require additional actuarial service. In the property and casualty insurance field, additional actuaries will be needed to make studies which are used in determining policy rate changes, and to justify these changes before State regulatory agencies. There will be continuing strong demand for actuaries capable of working with the electronic computers in widespread use by large insurance companies. Besides actuaries who will be needed to fill new positions, a few will have to be trained to replace those who retire, die, or transfer to other occupations.

HOW TO TAKE A TEST

I. YOU MUST PASS AN EXAMINATION

A. WHAT EVERY CANDIDATE SHOULD KNOW

Examination applicants often ask us for help in preparing for the written test. What can I study in advance? What kinds of questions will be asked? How will the test be given? How will the papers be graded?

As an applicant for a civil service examination, you may be wondering about some of these things. Our purpose here is to suggest effective methods of advance study and to describe civil service examinations.

Your chances for success on this examination can be increased if you know how to prepare. Those "pre-examination jitters" can be reduced if you know what to expect. You can even experience an adventure in good citizenship if you know why civil service exams are given.

B. WHY ARE CIVIL SERVICE EXAMINATIONS GIVEN?

Civil service examinations are important to you in two ways. As a citizen, you want public jobs filled by employees who know how to do their work. As a job seeker, you want a fair chance to compete for that job on an equal footing with other candidates. The best-known means of accomplishing this two-fold goal is the competitive examination.

Exams are widely publicized throughout the nation. They may be administered for jobs in federal, state, city, municipal, town or village governments or agencies.

Any citizen may apply, with some limitations, such as the age or residence of applicants. Your experience and education may be reviewed to see whether you meet the requirements for the particular examination. When these requirements exist, they are reasonable and applied consistently to all applicants. Thus, a competitive examination may cause you some uneasiness now, but it is your privilege and safeguard.

C. HOW ARE CIVIL SERVICE EXAMS DEVELOPED?

Examinations are carefully written by trained technicians who are specialists in the field known as "psychological measurement," in consultation with recognized authorities in the field of work that the test will cover. These experts recommend the subject matter areas or skills to be tested; only those knowledges or skills important to your success on the job are included. The most reliable books and source materials available are used as references. Together, the experts and technicians judge the difficulty level of the questions.

Test technicians know how to phrase questions so that the problem is clearly stated. Their ethics do not permit "trick" or "catch" questions. Questions may have been tried out on sample groups, or subjected to statistical analysis, to determine their usefulness.

Written tests are often used in combination with performance tests, ratings of training and experience, and oral interviews. All of these measures combine to form the best-known means of finding the right person for the right job.

II. HOW TO PASS THE WRITTEN TEST

A. NATURE OF THE EXAMINATION

To prepare intelligently for civil service examinations, you should know how they differ from school examinations you have taken. In school you were assigned certain definite pages to read or subjects to cover. The examination questions were quite detailed and usually emphasized memory. Civil service exams, on the other hand, try to discover your present ability to perform the duties of a position, plus your potentiality to learn these duties. In other words, a civil service exam attempts to predict how successful you will be. Questions cover such a broad area that they cannot be as minute and detailed as school exam questions.

In the public service similar kinds of work, or positions, are grouped together in one "class." This process is known as *position-classification*. All the positions in a class are paid according to the salary range for that class. One class title covers all of these positions, and they are all tested by the same examination.

B. FOUR BASIC STEPS

1) Study the announcement

How, then, can you know what subjects to study? Our best answer is: "Learn as much as possible about the class of positions for which you've applied." The exam will test the knowledge, skills and abilities needed to do the work.

Your most valuable source of information about the position you want is the official exam announcement. This announcement lists the training and experience qualifications. Check these standards and apply only if you come reasonably close to meeting them.

The brief description of the position in the examination announcement offers some clues to the subjects which will be tested. Think about the job itself. Review the duties in your mind. Can you perform them, or are there some in which you are rusty? Fill in the blank spots in your preparation.

Many jurisdictions preview the written test in the exam announcement by including a section called "Knowledge and Abilities Required," "Scope of the Examination," or some similar heading. Here you will find out specifically what fields will be tested.

2) Review your own background

Once you learn in general what the position is all about, and what you need to know to do the work, ask yourself which subjects you already know fairly well and which need improvement. You may wonder whether to concentrate on improving your strong areas or on building some background in your fields of weakness. When the announcement has specified "some knowledge" or "considerable knowledge," or has used adjectives like "beginning principles of…" or "advanced … methods," you can get a clue as to the number and difficulty of questions to be asked in any given field. More questions, and hence broader coverage, would be included for those subjects which are more important in the work. Now weigh your strengths and weaknesses against the job requirements and prepare accordingly.

3) Determine the level of the position

Another way to tell how intensively you should prepare is to understand the level of the job for which you are applying. Is it the entering level? In other words, is this the position in which beginners in a field of work are hired? Or is it an intermediate or advanced level? Sometimes this is indicated by such words as "Junior" or "Senior" in the class title. Other jurisdictions use Roman numerals to designate the level – Clerk I, Clerk II, for example. The word "Supervisor" sometimes appears in the title. If the level is not indicated by the title, check the description of duties. Will you be working under very close supervision, or will you have responsibility for independent decisions in this work?

4) Choose appropriate study materials

Now that you know the subjects to be examined and the relative amount of each subject to be covered, you can choose suitable study materials. For beginning level jobs, or even advanced ones, if you have a pronounced weakness in some aspect of your training, read a modern, standard textbook in that field. Be sure it is up to date and has general coverage. Such books are normally available at your library, and the librarian will be glad to help you locate one. For entry-level positions, questions of appropriate difficulty are chosen – neither highly advanced questions, nor those too simple. Such questions require careful thought but not advanced training.

If the position for which you are applying is technical or advanced, you will read more advanced, specialized material. If you are already familiar with the basic principles of your field, elementary textbooks would waste your time. Concentrate on advanced textbooks and technical periodicals. Think through the concepts and review difficult problems in your field.

These are all general sources. You can get more ideas on your own initiative, following these leads. For example, training manuals and publications of the government agency which employs workers in your field can be useful, particularly for technical and professional positions. A letter or visit to the government department involved may result in more specific study suggestions, and certainly will provide you with a more definite idea of the exact nature of the position you are seeking.

III. KINDS OF TESTS

Tests are used for purposes other than measuring knowledge and ability to perform specified duties. For some positions, it is equally important to test ability to make adjustments to new situations or to profit from training. In others, basic mental abilities not dependent on information are essential. Questions which test these things may not appear as pertinent to the duties of the position as those which test for knowledge and information. Yet they are often highly important parts of a fair examination. For very general questions, it is almost impossible to help you direct your study efforts. What we can do is to point out some of the more common of these general abilities needed in public service positions and describe some typical questions.

1) General information

Broad, general information has been found useful for predicting job success in some kinds of work. This is tested in a variety of ways, from vocabulary lists to questions about current events. Basic background in some field of work, such as

sociology or economics, may be sampled in a group of questions. Often these are principles which have become familiar to most persons through exposure rather than through formal training. It is difficult to advise you how to study for these questions; being alert to the world around you is our best suggestion.

2) Verbal ability

An example of an ability needed in many positions is verbal or language ability. Verbal ability is, in brief, the ability to use and understand words. Vocabulary and grammar tests are typical measures of this ability. Reading comprehension or paragraph interpretation questions are common in many kinds of civil service tests. You are given a paragraph of written material and asked to find its central meaning.

3) Numerical ability

Number skills can be tested by the familiar arithmetic problem, by checking paired lists of numbers to see which are alike and which are different, or by interpreting charts and graphs. In the latter test, a graph may be printed in the test booklet which you are asked to use as the basis for answering questions.

4) Observation

A popular test for law-enforcement positions is the observation test. A picture is shown to you for several minutes, then taken away. Questions about the picture test your ability to observe both details and larger elements.

5) Following directions

In many positions in the public service, the employee must be able to carry out written instructions dependably and accurately. You may be given a chart with several columns, each column listing a variety of information. The questions require you to carry out directions involving the information given in the chart.

6) Skills and aptitudes

Performance tests effectively measure some manual skills and aptitudes. When the skill is one in which you are trained, such as typing or shorthand, you can practice. These tests are often very much like those given in business school or high school courses. For many of the other skills and aptitudes, however, no short-time preparation can be made. Skills and abilities natural to you or that you have developed throughout your lifetime are being tested.

Many of the general questions just described provide all the data needed to answer the questions and ask you to use your reasoning ability to find the answers. Your best preparation for these tests, as well as for tests of facts and ideas, is to be at your physical and mental best. You, no doubt, have your own methods of getting into an exam-taking mood and keeping "in shape." The next section lists some ideas on this subject.

IV. KINDS OF QUESTIONS

Only rarely is the "essay" question, which you answer in narrative form, used in civil service tests. Civil service tests are usually of the short-answer type. Full instructions for answering these questions will be given to you at the examination. But in

case this is your first experience with short-answer questions and separate answer sheets, here is what you need to know:

1) Multiple-choice Questions

Most popular of the short-answer questions is the "multiple choice" or "best answer" question. It can be used, for example, to test for factual knowledge, ability to solve problems or judgment in meeting situations found at work.

A multiple-choice question is normally one of three types—

- It can begin with an incomplete statement followed by several possible endings. You are to find the one ending which *best* completes the statement, although some of the others may not be entirely wrong.
- It can also be a complete statement in the form of a question which is answered by choosing one of the statements listed.
- It can be in the form of a problem – again you select the best answer.

Here is an example of a multiple-choice question with a discussion which should give you some clues as to the method for choosing the right answer:

When an employee has a complaint about his assignment, the action which will *best* help him overcome his difficulty is to
  A. discuss his difficulty with his coworkers
  B. take the problem to the head of the organization
  C. take the problem to the person who gave him the assignment
  D. say nothing to anyone about his complaint

In answering this question, you should study each of the choices to find which is best. Consider choice "A" – Certainly an employee may discuss his complaint with fellow employees, but no change or improvement can result, and the complaint remains unresolved. Choice "B" is a poor choice since the head of the organization probably does not know what assignment you have been given, and taking your problem to him is known as "going over the head" of the supervisor. The supervisor, or person who made the assignment, is the person who can clarify it or correct any injustice. Choice "C" is, therefore, correct. To say nothing, as in choice "D," is unwise. Supervisors have and interest in knowing the problems employees are facing, and the employee is seeking a solution to his problem.

2) True/False Questions

The "true/false" or "right/wrong" form of question is sometimes used. Here a complete statement is given. Your job is to decide whether the statement is right or wrong.

SAMPLE: A roaming cell-phone call to a nearby city costs less than a non-roaming call to a distant city.

This statement is wrong, or false, since roaming calls are more expensive.
This is not a complete list of all possible question forms, although most of the others are variations of these common types. You will always get complete directions for

answering questions. Be sure you understand *how* to mark your answers – ask questions until you do.

V. RECORDING YOUR ANSWERS

Computer terminals are used more and more today for many different kinds of exams.

For an examination with very few applicants, you may be told to record your answers in the test booklet itself. Separate answer sheets are much more common. If this separate answer sheet is to be scored by machine – and this is often the case – it is highly important that you mark your answers correctly in order to get credit.

An electronic scoring machine is often used in civil service offices because of the speed with which papers can be scored. Machine-scored answer sheets must be marked with a pencil, which will be given to you. This pencil has a high graphite content which responds to the electronic scoring machine. As a matter of fact, stray dots may register as answers, so do not let your pencil rest on the answer sheet while you are pondering the correct answer. Also, if your pencil lead breaks or is otherwise defective, ask for another.

Since the answer sheet will be dropped in a slot in the scoring machine, be careful not to bend the corners or get the paper crumpled.

The answer sheet normally has five vertical columns of numbers, with 30 numbers to a column. These numbers correspond to the question numbers in your test booklet. After each number, going across the page are four or five pairs of dotted lines. These short dotted lines have small letters or numbers above them. The first two pairs may also have a "T" or "F" above the letters. This indicates that the first two pairs only are to be used if the questions are of the true-false type. If the questions are multiple choice, disregard the "T" and "F" and pay attention only to the small letters or numbers.

Answer your questions in the manner of the sample that follows:

> 32. The largest city in the United States is
>   A. Washington, D.C.
>   B. New York City
>   C. Chicago
>   D. Detroit
>   E. San Francisco

> 1) Choose the answer you think is best. (New York City is the largest, so "B" is correct.)
> 2) Find the row of dotted lines numbered the same as the question you are answering. (Find row number 32)
> 3) Find the pair of dotted lines corresponding to the answer. (Find the pair of lines under the mark "B.")
> 4) Make a solid black mark between the dotted lines.

VI. BEFORE THE TEST

Common sense will help you find procedures to follow to get ready for an examination. Too many of us, however, overlook these sensible measures. Indeed,

nervousness and fatigue have been found to be the most serious reasons why applicants fail to do their best on civil service tests. Here is a list of reminders:

- Begin your preparation early – Don't wait until the last minute to go scurrying around for books and materials or to find out what the position is all about.
- Prepare continuously – An hour a night for a week is better than an all-night cram session. This has been definitely established. What is more, a night a week for a month will return better dividends than crowding your study into a shorter period of time.
- Locate the place of the exam – You have been sent a notice telling you when and where to report for the examination. If the location is in a different town or otherwise unfamiliar to you, it would be well to inquire the best route and learn something about the building.
- Relax the night before the test – Allow your mind to rest. Do not study at all that night. Plan some mild recreation or diversion; then go to bed early and get a good night's sleep.
- Get up early enough to make a leisurely trip to the place for the test – This way unforeseen events, traffic snarls, unfamiliar buildings, etc. will not upset you.
- Dress comfortably – A written test is not a fashion show. You will be known by number and not by name, so wear something comfortable.
- Leave excess paraphernalia at home – Shopping bags and odd bundles will get in your way. You need bring only the items mentioned in the official notice you received; usually everything you need is provided. Do not bring reference books to the exam. They will only confuse those last minutes and be taken away from you when in the test room.
- Arrive somewhat ahead of time – If because of transportation schedules you must get there very early, bring a newspaper or magazine to take your mind off yourself while waiting.
- Locate the examination room – When you have found the proper room, you will be directed to the seat or part of the room where you will sit. Sometimes you are given a sheet of instructions to read while you are waiting. Do not fill out any forms until you are told to do so; just read them and be prepared.
- Relax and prepare to listen to the instructions
- If you have any physical problem that may keep you from doing your best, be sure to tell the test administrator. If you are sick or in poor health, you really cannot do your best on the exam. You can come back and take the test some other time.

VII. AT THE TEST

The day of the test is here and you have the test booklet in your hand. The temptation to get going is very strong. Caution! There is more to success than knowing the right answers. You must know how to identify your papers and understand variations in the type of short-answer question used in this particular examination. Follow these suggestions for maximum results from your efforts:

1) Cooperate with the monitor

The test administrator has a duty to create a situation in which you can be as much at ease as possible. He will give instructions, tell you when to begin, check to see that you are marking your answer sheet correctly, and so on. He is not there to guard you, although he will see that your competitors do not take unfair advantage. He wants to help you do your best.

2) Listen to all instructions

Don't jump the gun! Wait until you understand all directions. In most civil service tests you get more time than you need to answer the questions. So don't be in a hurry. Read each word of instructions until you clearly understand the meaning. Study the examples, listen to all announcements and follow directions. Ask questions if you do not understand what to do.

3) Identify your papers

Civil service exams are usually identified by number only. You will be assigned a number; you must not put your name on your test papers. Be sure to copy your number correctly. Since more than one exam may be given, copy your exact examination title.

4) Plan your time

Unless you are told that a test is a "speed" or "rate of work" test, speed itself is usually not important. Time enough to answer all the questions will be provided, but this does not mean that you have all day. An overall time limit has been set. Divide the total time (in minutes) by the number of questions to determine the approximate time you have for each question.

5) Do not linger over difficult questions

If you come across a difficult question, mark it with a paper clip (useful to have along) and come back to it when you have been through the booklet. One caution if you do this – be sure to skip a number on your answer sheet as well. Check often to be sure that you have not lost your place and that you are marking in the row numbered the same as the question you are answering.

6) Read the questions

Be sure you know what the question asks! Many capable people are unsuccessful because they failed to *read* the questions correctly.

7) Answer all questions

Unless you have been instructed that a penalty will be deducted for incorrect answers, it is better to guess than to omit a question.

8) Speed tests

It is often better NOT to guess on speed tests. It has been found that on timed tests people are tempted to spend the last few seconds before time is called in marking answers at random – without even reading them – in the hope of picking up a few extra points. To discourage this practice, the instructions may warn you that your score will be "corrected" for guessing. That is, a penalty will be applied. The incorrect answers will be deducted from the correct ones, or some other penalty formula will be used.

9) Review your answers

If you finish before time is called, go back to the questions you guessed or omitted to give them further thought. Review other answers if you have time.

10) Return your test materials

If you are ready to leave before others have finished or time is called, take ALL your materials to the monitor and leave quietly. Never take any test material with you. The monitor can discover whose papers are not complete, and taking a test booklet may be grounds for disqualification.

VIII. EXAMINATION TECHNIQUES

1) Read the general instructions carefully. These are usually printed on the first page of the exam booklet. As a rule, these instructions refer to the timing of the examination; the fact that you should not start work until the signal and must stop work at a signal, etc. If there are any *special* instructions, such as a choice of questions to be answered, make sure that you note this instruction carefully.

2) When you are ready to start work on the examination, that is as soon as the signal has been given, read the instructions to each question booklet, underline any key words or phrases, such as *least, best, outline, describe* and the like. In this way you will tend to answer as requested rather than discover on reviewing your paper that you *listed without describing*, that you selected the *worst* choice rather than the *best* choice, etc.

3) If the examination is of the objective or multiple-choice type – that is, each question will also give a series of possible answers: A, B, C or D, and you are called upon to select the best answer and write the letter next to that answer on your answer paper – it is advisable to start answering each question in turn. There may be anywhere from 50 to 100 such questions in the three or four hours allotted and you can see how much time would be taken if you read through all the questions before beginning to answer any. Furthermore, if you come across a question or group of questions which you know would be difficult to answer, it would undoubtedly affect your handling of all the other questions.

4) If the examination is of the essay type and contains but a few questions, it is a moot point as to whether you should read all the questions before starting to answer any one. Of course, if you are given a choice – say five out of seven and the like – then it is essential to read all the questions so you can eliminate the two that are most difficult. If, however, you are asked to answer all the questions, there may be danger in trying to answer the easiest one first because you may find that you will spend too much time on it. The best technique is to answer the first question, then proceed to the second, etc.

5) Time your answers. Before the exam begins, write down the time it started, then add the time allowed for the examination and write down the time it must be completed, then divide the time available somewhat as follows:

- If 3-1/2 hours are allowed, that would be 210 minutes. If you have 80 objective-type questions, that would be an average of 2-1/2 minutes per question. Allow yourself no more than 2 minutes per question, or a total of 160 minutes, which will permit about 50 minutes to review.
- If for the time allotment of 210 minutes there are 7 essay questions to answer, that would average about 30 minutes a question. Give yourself only 25 minutes per question so that you have about 35 minutes to review.

6) The most important instruction is to *read each question* and make sure you know what is wanted. The second most important instruction is to *time yourself properly* so that you answer every question. The third most important instruction is to *answer every question*. Guess if you have to but include something for each question. Remember that you will receive no credit for a blank and will probably receive some credit if you write something in answer to an essay question. If you guess a letter – say "B" for a multiple-choice question – you may have guessed right. If you leave a blank as an answer to a multiple-choice question, the examiners may respect your feelings but it will not add a point to your score. Some exams may penalize you for wrong answers, so in such cases *only*, you may not want to guess unless you have some basis for your answer.

7) Suggestions
   a. Objective-type questions
      1. Examine the question booklet for proper sequence of pages and questions
      2. Read all instructions carefully
      3. Skip any question which seems too difficult; return to it after all other questions have been answered
      4. Apportion your time properly; do not spend too much time on any single question or group of questions
      5. Note and underline key words – *all, most, fewest, least, best, worst, same, opposite,* etc.
      6. Pay particular attention to negatives
      7. Note unusual option, e.g., unduly long, short, complex, different or similar in content to the body of the question
      8. Observe the use of "hedging" words – *probably, may, most likely,* etc.
      9. Make sure that your answer is put next to the same number as the question
      10. Do not second-guess unless you have good reason to believe the second answer is definitely more correct
      11. Cross out original answer if you decide another answer is more accurate; do not erase until you are ready to hand your paper in
      12. Answer all questions; guess unless instructed otherwise
      13. Leave time for review

   b. Essay questions
      1. Read each question carefully
      2. Determine exactly what is wanted. Underline key words or phrases.
      3. Decide on outline or paragraph answer

4. Include many different points and elements unless asked to develop any one or two points or elements
5. Show impartiality by giving pros and cons unless directed to select one side only
6. Make and write down any assumptions you find necessary to answer the questions
7. Watch your English, grammar, punctuation and choice of words
8. Time your answers; don't crowd material

8) Answering the essay question

Most essay questions can be answered by framing the specific response around several key words or ideas. Here are a few such key words or ideas:

M's: manpower, materials, methods, money, management
P's: purpose, program, policy, plan, procedure, practice, problems, pitfalls, personnel, public relations
    a. Six basic steps in handling problems:
      1. Preliminary plan and background development
      2. Collect information, data and facts
      3. Analyze and interpret information, data and facts
      4. Analyze and develop solutions as well as make recommendations
      5. Prepare report and sell recommendations
      6. Install recommendations and follow up effectiveness

    b. Pitfalls to avoid
      1. *Taking things for granted* – A statement of the situation does not necessarily imply that each of the elements is necessarily true; for example, a complaint may be invalid and biased so that all that can be taken for granted is that a complaint has been registered
      2. *Considering only one side of a situation* – Wherever possible, indicate several alternatives and then point out the reasons you selected the best one
      3. *Failing to indicate follow up* – Whenever your answer indicates action on your part, make certain that you will take proper follow-up action to see how successful your recommendations, procedures or actions turn out to be
      4. *Taking too long in answering any single question* – Remember to time your answers properly

IX. AFTER THE TEST

Scoring procedures differ in detail among civil service jurisdictions although the general principles are the same. Whether the papers are hand-scored or graded by machine we have described, they are nearly always graded by number. That is, the person who marks the paper knows only the number – never the name – of the applicant. Not until all the papers have been graded will they be matched with names. If other tests, such as training and experience or oral interview ratings have been given, scores will be combined. Different parts of the examination usually have different weights. For example, the written test might count 60 percent of the final grade, and a rating of training and experience 40 percent. In many jurisdictions, veterans will have a certain number of points added to their grades.

After the final grade has been determined, the names are placed in grade order and an eligible list is established. There are various methods for resolving ties between those who get the same final grade – probably the most common is to place first the name of the person whose application was received first. Job offers are made from the eligible list in the order the names appear on it. You will be notified of your grade and your rank as soon as all these computations have been made. This will be done as rapidly as possible.

People who are found to meet the requirements in the announcement are called "eligibles." Their names are put on a list of eligible candidates. An eligible's chances of getting a job depend on how high he stands on this list and how fast agencies are filling jobs from the list.

When a job is to be filled from a list of eligibles, the agency asks for the names of people on the list of eligibles for that job. When the civil service commission receives this request, it sends to the agency the names of the three people highest on this list. Or, if the job to be filled has specialized requirements, the office sends the agency the names of the top three persons who meet these requirements from the general list.

The appointing officer makes a choice from among the three people whose names were sent to him. If the selected person accepts the appointment, the names of the others are put back on the list to be considered for future openings.

That is the rule in hiring from all kinds of eligible lists, whether they are for typist, carpenter, chemist, or something else. For every vacancy, the appointing officer has his choice of any one of the top three eligibles on the list. This explains why the person whose name is on top of the list sometimes does not get an appointment when some of the persons lower on the list do. If the appointing officer chooses the second or third eligible, the No. 1 eligible does not get a job at once, but stays on the list until he is appointed or the list is terminated.

X. HOW TO PASS THE INTERVIEW TEST

The examination for which you applied requires an oral interview test. You have already taken the written test and you are now being called for the interview test – the final part of the formal examination.

You may think that it is not possible to prepare for an interview test and that there are no procedures to follow during an interview. Our purpose is to point out some things you can do in advance that will help you and some good rules to follow and pitfalls to avoid while you are being interviewed.

What is an interview supposed to test?
The written examination is designed to test the technical knowledge and competence of the candidate; the oral is designed to evaluate intangible qualities, not readily measured otherwise, and to establish a list showing the relative fitness of each candidate – as measured against his competitors – for the position sought. Scoring is not on the basis of "right" and "wrong," but on a sliding scale of values ranging from "not passable" to "outstanding." As a matter of fact, it is possible to achieve a relatively low score without a single "incorrect" answer because of evident weakness in the qualities being measured.

Occasionally, an examination may consist entirely of an oral test – either an individual or a group oral. In such cases, information is sought concerning the technical knowledges and abilities of the candidate, since there has been no written examination for this purpose. More commonly, however, an oral test is used to supplement a written examination.

Who conducts interviews?

The composition of oral boards varies among different jurisdictions. In nearly all, a representative of the personnel department serves as chairman. One of the members of the board may be a representative of the department in which the candidate would work. In some cases, "outside experts" are used, and, frequently, a businessman or some other representative of the general public is asked to serve. Labor and management or other special groups may be represented. The aim is to secure the services of experts in the appropriate field.

However the board is composed, it is a good idea (and not at all improper or unethical) to ascertain in advance of the interview who the members are and what groups they represent. When you are introduced to them, you will have some idea of their backgrounds and interests, and at least you will not stutter and stammer over their names.

What should be done before the interview?

While knowledge about the board members is useful and takes some of the surprise element out of the interview, there is other preparation which is more substantive. It *is* possible to prepare for an oral interview – in several ways:

1) Keep a copy of your application and review it carefully before the interview

This may be the only document before the oral board, and the starting point of the interview. Know what education and experience you have listed there, and the sequence and dates of all of it. Sometimes the board will ask you to review the highlights of your experience for them; you should not have to hem and haw doing it.

2) Study the class specification and the examination announcement

Usually, the oral board has one or both of these to guide them. The qualities, characteristics or knowledges required by the position sought are stated in these documents. They offer valuable clues as to the nature of the oral interview. For example, if the job involves supervisory responsibilities, the announcement will usually indicate that knowledge of modern supervisory methods and the qualifications of the candidate as a supervisor will be tested. If so, you can expect such questions, frequently in the form of a hypothetical situation which you are expected to solve. NEVER go into an oral without knowledge of the duties and responsibilities of the job you seek.

3) Think through each qualification required

Try to visualize the kind of questions you would ask if you were a board member. How well could you answer them? Try especially to appraise your own knowledge and background in each area, *measured against the job sought*, and identify any areas in which you are weak. Be critical and realistic – do not flatter yourself.

4) Do some general reading in areas in which you feel you may be weak

For example, if the job involves supervision and your past experience has NOT, some general reading in supervisory methods and practices, particularly in the field of human relations, might be useful. Do NOT study agency procedures or detailed manuals. The oral board will be testing your understanding and capacity, not your memory.

5) Get a good night's sleep and watch your general health and mental attitude

You will want a clear head at the interview. Take care of a cold or any other minor ailment, and of course, no hangovers.

What should be done on the day of the interview?

Now comes the day of the interview itself. Give yourself plenty of time to get there. Plan to arrive somewhat ahead of the scheduled time, particularly if your appointment is in the fore part of the day. If a previous candidate fails to appear, the board might be ready for you a bit early. By early afternoon an oral board is almost invariably behind schedule if there are many candidates, and you may have to wait. Take along a book or magazine to read, or your application to review, but leave any extraneous material in the waiting room when you go in for your interview. In any event, relax and compose yourself.

The matter of dress is important. The board is forming impressions about you – from your experience, your manners, your attitude, and your appearance. Give your personal appearance careful attention. Dress your best, but not your flashiest. Choose conservative, appropriate clothing, and be sure it is immaculate. This is a business interview, and your appearance should indicate that you regard it as such. Besides, being well groomed and properly dressed will help boost your confidence.

Sooner or later, someone will call your name and escort you into the interview room. *This is it.* From here on you are on your own. It is too late for any more preparation. But remember, you asked for this opportunity to prove your fitness, and you are here because your request was granted.

What happens when you go in?

The usual sequence of events will be as follows: The clerk (who is often the board stenographer) will introduce you to the chairman of the oral board, who will introduce you to the other members of the board. Acknowledge the introductions before you sit down. Do not be surprised if you find a microphone facing you or a stenotypist sitting by. Oral interviews are usually recorded in the event of an appeal or other review.

Usually the chairman of the board will open the interview by reviewing the highlights of your education and work experience from your application – primarily for the benefit of the other members of the board, as well as to get the material into the record. Do not interrupt or comment unless there is an error or significant misinterpretation; if that is the case, do not hesitate. But do not quibble about insignificant matters. Also, he will usually ask you some question about your education, experience or your present job – partly to get you to start talking and to establish the interviewing "rapport." He may start the actual questioning, or turn it over to one of the other members. Frequently, each member undertakes the questioning on a particular area, one in which he is perhaps most competent, so you can expect each member to participate in the examination. Because time is limited, you may also expect some rather abrupt switches in the direction the questioning takes, so do not be upset by it. Normally, a board member will not pursue a single line of questioning unless he discovers a particular strength or weakness.

After each member has participated, the chairman will usually ask whether any member has any further questions, then will ask you if you have anything you wish to add. Unless you are expecting this question, it may floor you. Worse, it may start you off on an extended, extemporaneous speech. The board is not usually seeking more information. The question is principally to offer you a last opportunity to present further qualifications or to indicate that you have nothing to add. So, if you feel that a significant qualification or characteristic has been overlooked, it is proper to point it out in a sentence or so. Do not compliment the board on the thoroughness of their examination – they have been sketchy, and you know it. If you wish, merely say, "No thank you, I have nothing further to add." This is a point where you can "talk yourself out" of a good impression or fail to present an important bit of information. Remember, *you close the interview yourself.*

The chairman will then say, "That is all, Mr. _____, thank you." Do not be startled; the interview is over, and quicker than you think. Thank him, gather your belongings and take your leave. Save your sigh of relief for the other side of the door.

How to put your best foot forward
Throughout this entire process, you may feel that the board individually and collectively is trying to pierce your defenses, seek out your hidden weaknesses and embarrass and confuse you. Actually, this is not true. They are obliged to make an appraisal of your qualifications for the job you are seeking, and they want to see you in your best light. Remember, they must interview all candidates and a non-cooperative candidate may become a failure in spite of their best efforts to bring out his qualifications. Here are 15 suggestions that will help you:

1) Be natural – Keep your attitude confident, not cocky
If you are not confident that you can do the job, do not expect the board to be. Do not apologize for your weaknesses, try to bring out your strong points. The board is interested in a positive, not negative, presentation. Cockiness will antagonize any board member and make him wonder if you are covering up a weakness by a false show of strength.

2) Get comfortable, but don't lounge or sprawl
Sit erectly but not stiffly. A careless posture may lead the board to conclude that you are careless in other things, or at least that you are not impressed by the importance of the occasion. Either conclusion is natural, even if incorrect. Do not fuss with your clothing, a pencil or an ashtray. Your hands may occasionally be useful to emphasize a point; do not let them become a point of distraction.

3) Do not wisecrack or make small talk
This is a serious situation, and your attitude should show that you consider it as such. Further, the time of the board is limited – they do not want to waste it, and neither should you.

4) Do not exaggerate your experience or abilities
In the first place, from information in the application or other interviews and sources, the board may know more about you than you think. Secondly, you probably will not get away with it. An experienced board is rather adept at spotting such a situation, so do not take the chance.

5) If you know a board member, do not make a point of it, yet do not hide it

Certainly you are not fooling him, and probably not the other members of the board. Do not try to take advantage of your acquaintanceship – it will probably do you little good.

6) Do not dominate the interview

Let the board do that. They will give you the clues – do not assume that you have to do all the talking. Realize that the board has a number of questions to ask you, and do not try to take up all the interview time by showing off your extensive knowledge of the answer to the first one.

7) Be attentive

You only have 20 minutes or so, and you should keep your attention at its sharpest throughout. When a member is addressing a problem or question to you, give him your undivided attention. Address your reply principally to him, but do not exclude the other board members.

8) Do not interrupt

A board member may be stating a problem for you to analyze. He will ask you a question when the time comes. Let him state the problem, and wait for the question.

9) Make sure you understand the question

Do not try to answer until you are sure what the question is. If it is not clear, restate it in your own words or ask the board member to clarify it for you. However, do not haggle about minor elements.

10) Reply promptly but not hastily

A common entry on oral board rating sheets is "candidate responded readily," or "candidate hesitated in replies." Respond as promptly and quickly as you can, but do not jump to a hasty, ill-considered answer.

11) Do not be peremptory in your answers

A brief answer is proper – but do not fire your answer back. That is a losing game from your point of view. The board member can probably ask questions much faster than you can answer them.

12) Do not try to create the answer you think the board member wants

He is interested in what kind of mind you have and how it works – not in playing games. Furthermore, he can usually spot this practice and will actually grade you down on it.

13) Do not switch sides in your reply merely to agree with a board member

Frequently, a member will take a contrary position merely to draw you out and to see if you are willing and able to defend your point of view. Do not start a debate, yet do not surrender a good position. If a position is worth taking, it is worth defending.

14) Do not be afraid to admit an error in judgment if you are shown to be wrong

The board knows that you are forced to reply without any opportunity for careful consideration. Your answer may be demonstrably wrong. If so, admit it and get on with the interview.

15) Do not dwell at length on your present job

The opening question may relate to your present assignment. Answer the question but do not go into an extended discussion. You are being examined for a *new* job, not your present one. As a matter of fact, try to phrase ALL your answers in terms of the job for which you are being examined.

Basis of Rating

Probably you will forget most of these "do's" and "don'ts" when you walk into the oral interview room. Even remembering them all will not ensure you a passing grade. Perhaps you did not have the qualifications in the first place. But remembering them will help you to put your best foot forward, without treading on the toes of the board members.

Rumor and popular opinion to the contrary notwithstanding, an oral board wants you to make the best appearance possible. They know you are under pressure – but they also want to see how you respond to it as a guide to what your reaction would be under the pressures of the job you seek. They will be influenced by the degree of poise you display, the personal traits you show and the manner in which you respond.

ABOUT THIS BOOK

This book contains tests divided into Examination Sections. Go through each test, answering every question in the margin. At the end of each test look at the answer key and check your answers. On the ones you got wrong, look at the right answer choice and learn. Do not fill in the answers first. Do not memorize the questions and answers, but understand the answer and principles involved. On your test, the questions will likely be different from the samples. Questions are changed and new ones added. If you understand these past questions you should have success with any changes that arise. Tests may consist of several types of questions. We have additional books on each subject should more study be advisable or necessary for you. Finally, the more you study, the better prepared you will be. This book is intended to be the last thing you study before you walk into the examination room. Prior study of relevant texts is also recommended. NLC publishes some of these in our Fundamental Series. Knowledge and good sense are important factors in passing your exam. Good luck also helps. So now study this Passbook, absorb the material contained within and take that knowledge into the examination. Then do your best to pass that exam.

EXAMINATION SECTION

DIRECTIONS: Each question or incomplete statement is followed by several suggested answers or completions. Select the one that BEST answers the question or completes the statement. *PRINT THE LETTER OF THE CORRECT ANSWER IN THE SPACE AT THE RIGHT.*

1. If $y = \dfrac{1}{x-2}$, $x \neq 2$, for what value of x is $y^2 = -2y^3$?

    A. -4   B. -2   C. -1/2   D. 0   E. No value

1____

2. If P and Q are constants such that

$$\frac{P}{e^x - 1} + \frac{Q}{e^x + 2} = \frac{2e^x + 3}{(e^x - 1)(e^x + 2)},$$

    then (P + Q) =

    A. -2   B. -4/3   C. 2/3   D. 4/3   E. 2

2____

3. If $x^2 + 2xy + y^2 = 4$, then $\dfrac{dy}{dx} =$

    A. -1   B. 1   C. 2x + 2y   D. 4x + 4y
    E. None of these

3____

4. If $\int x^n \cos x\, dx \equiv x^n \sin x - \int M dx$, then M =

    A. $(n-1)x^{n-1} \sin x$ B. $nx^{n-1} \sin x$

    C. $x^n \sin x$ D. $x^{n-1} \cos x$ E. $nx^{n-1} \cos x$

4____

5. The points $(1, y_1)$ and $(-1, y_2)$ lie on the curve
$y = 4x^4 + px^3 + qx^2 + rx + 5$. If $y_1 + y_2 = 10$, what is the value of q?

    A. -9   B. -4   C. -1   D. 5
    E. It cannot be determined from the information given

5____

6. If $f(x) = x - \dfrac{1}{x}$, which of the following are correct?

    I. $f(-x) = -f(x)$

    II. $f(\dfrac{1}{x}) = -f(x)$

    III. $f(x^2) = -f(x)f(-x)$

6____

A. I only   B. I and II only   C. I and III only
D. II and III only   E. I, II, and III

7. If the point $(3,y)$ lies on the line joining $(0,3/2)$ and $(9/4,0)$, then $y =$ 7_____

     A. -7/2   B. -2   C. -1/2   D. 1/2   E. 3/2

8. If $dx = 3t^2 dt$ and if $x = 3$ when $t = 1$, what is the value of x when $t = 2$?   8_____

     A. 6   B. 8   C. 10   D. 12   E. 24

9. If $f(x) = \dfrac{x+1}{x}$, $x \neq 0$, and if $f(g(x)) = x$, then $g(x) =$ 9_____

     A. $\dfrac{x^2}{x+1}$ B. $\dfrac{x}{x-1}$ C. $\dfrac{x}{x+1}$ D. $\dfrac{1}{1-x}$ E. $\dfrac{1}{x-1}$

10. The slope of the tangent to the curve $2x^3 - x^2y^2 + 4y^3 = 16$ at the point $(2,1)$ is   10_____

     A. -5   B. -16/5   C. -5/16   D. 5/2   E. 6

11. If $2x + iy - 3y + 2i = 0$, where x and y are real and $i = \sqrt{-1}$, solve for x and y.   11_____

     A. $\begin{matrix} x = -3 \\ y = -2 \end{matrix}$ B. $\begin{matrix} x = 0 \\ y = 0 \end{matrix}$ C. $\begin{matrix} x - 1 \\ y = -2/3 \end{matrix}$ D. $\begin{matrix} x = 3 \\ y = -2 \end{matrix}$ E. $\begin{matrix} x = 3 \\ y = 2 \end{matrix}$

12. The first and second terms of a geometric series are x^{-4} and xt, respectively. If x^{52} is the eighth term of the series, $t =$ 12_____

     A. 5/2   B. 24/7   C. 4   D. 11   E. 12

13. If $x = 1 - e^t$ and $y = 1 + e^{-t}$, then an expression for y as a function of x is   13_____

     A. $y = x$ B. $y = 2 - x$ C. $y = \dfrac{2-x}{x-1}$ D. $y = \dfrac{x-2}{x-1}$ E. $y = \dfrac{x}{x-1}$

14. Given $y = x^3 - 8x + 7$ and $x = f(t)$. If $x = 3$ when $t = 0$ and if $f'(0) = 2$, what is dy/dt when $t = 0$?   14_____

     A. -8   B. -4   C. 19/2   D. 19   E. 38

15. A farmer estimates that if he digs his potatoes now he will have 100 bushels, which he can sell at \$1.50 per bushel. If he expects his crop to increase to 10 bushels per week, but the price to drop \$0.05 per bushel per week, in how many weeks should he sell to realize the MAXIMUM amount for his potato crop?   15_____

     A. 3 1/3   B. 5   C. 10   D. 15   E. 20

16. A particle moves along the X-axis so that its position is given by $x = 2t^3 - 3t^2$ at time t seconds. What is the complete time interval during which the particle will be on the negative half of the axis?   16_____

A.   0<t<2/3   B.   0<t<1   C.   0<t<3/2   D.   4<t<1   E.   1<1/2<3/2

17. The radius r of a cylinder is increasing 1/2 inch per minute and the altitude h is increasing 1/8 inch per minute. How many cubic inches per minute is the volume of the cylinder increasing when r = 4 inches and h = 6 inches?

17____

A. 3π B. 14π C. 16π D. 24π E. 26π

18. $\lim\limits_{t\to\infty} t^3 e^{-t} =$

18____

A.   -3   B.   0   C.   3e   D.   6e   E. ∞

19. If F is a function such that

19____

$$F(0) = 2$$
$$\{ F(l) = 3$$
$$F(n+2)=2F(n) - F(n+l),$$

then F(5) =

A.   -7   B.   -3   C.   7   D.   10   E.   13

20. An equation of the tangent to the curve

20____

$$\{ \begin{matrix} x = t^3 - 4 \\ y = 2t^2 + 1 \end{matrix} \}$$

at the point where t = 2 is

A.   2x - 3y - 19 = 0   B.   2x - 3y + 19 = 0
C.   3x - 2y - 6 = 0   D.   3x - 2y + 6 = 0
E.   3x + 2y - 6 = 0

21. Using a Maclaurin series, approximate the value of $e^{-1/5}$ to the nearest 0.01.

21____

A.   0.68   B.   0.78   C.   0.82   D.   1.18   E.   1.22

22. If $\phi (x,y,a) = \sin x + x \cos y + x \tan z$, which of the following are identically equal to zero?

22____

I. $\dfrac{\partial^2 \phi}{\partial x \partial y}$ II. $\dfrac{\partial^2 \phi}{\partial z^2}$ III. $\dfrac{\partial^2 \phi}{\partial y \partial z}$

A.   I only   B.   II only   C.   III only
D.   I and III only   E.   II and III only

23. If $\log_8 m \to \log_8 1/6 = 2/3$, then m =

23____

A.   1/2   B.   2/3   C.   23/6   D.   4   E.   24

24. What is the MAXIMUM slope of the curve $y = -x^3 + 3x^2 + 9x - 27$?

24____

A.   -32   B.   -16   C.   0   D.   6   E.   12

25. What is the coefficient of x^{-3} in the binomial expansion of $(x-\frac{m}{x})^{11}$?

25____

    A. $-924m^7$ B. $-495m^4$ C. $-330m^7$ D. $-330m^8$ E. $165m^8$

26. What is the volume of the solid generated by revolving the first-quadrant area bounded by the coordinate axes and the curve $y^2 + 6x = 36$ about the x-axis?

26____

    A. 54π B. 72π C. 108π D. 144π E. 216π

27. The area bounded by the curve $y = x^2$, the x-axis, and the line x = 21/3 is divided into two equal areas by the line x = k. What is the value of k?

27____

    A. 1   B. $2^{-2/3}$ C. $2^{1/6}$ D. $2^{1/3}$ E. $2^{2/3}-1$

28. $\lim\limits_{x \to \infty} \dfrac{2\tan 2x}{1-\cos x} =$

28____

    A. 0   B. 1/2   C. 1   D. 2   E. ∞

29. A parabola with its vertex at the origin and its axis along the Y-axis contains the point (4,4). What is the y-coordinate of the point on this parabola whose x-coor-dinate is 6?

29____

    A. $\dfrac{\sqrt{6}}{2}$ B. $2\sqrt{6}$ C. 6   D. 9   E. 24

30. If $4x^2 + 8xy + ky^2 = 9$ is the equation of a pair of straight lines, then k =

30____

    A. 0   B. 1   C. 3/2   D. 9/4   E. 4

31. An equation of the perpendicular bisector of the line segment with end points (1,5) and (-3,2) is

31____

    A. 3x - 4y + 17 = 0   B. 4x + 3y - 13 = 0
    C. 8x - 6y + 29 = 0   D. 8x + 6y - 13 = 0
    E. 8x + 6y + 13 = 0

32. Find the derivative of

32____

$$y = \frac{x \cos x}{1+e^x} \quad \text{at } x = 0.$$

    A. -1/4   B. 0   C. 1/4   D. 1/2   E. 1

33. $(1-\frac{1}{4})(1-1/5)\ldots\ldots(1-\frac{1}{n+2})(1-\frac{1}{n+3}) =$

33____

    A. $\dfrac{1}{n+3}$ B. $\dfrac{3}{n+3}$ C. $\dfrac{3(n+2)}{n+3}$ D. $\dfrac{4(n+2)}{n+3}$

E. $\dfrac{4}{(n+2)(n+3)}$

34. If $i = \sqrt{-1}$, $(1+i)^9$

34____

    A. $-16 + 16i$ B. $16 - 16i$ C. $16 + 16i$
    D. $-512 + 512i$ E. $512 + 512i$

35. If $\log_k x \log_5 k = 3$, then $x =$

35____

    A. $2k/125$ B. $5k^3$ C. 15 D. 125 E. 243

36. In what interval is the infinite series

36____

    $1 + 2(x-3) + 3(x-3)^2 + 4(x-3)^3 + \ldots$
convergent?

    A. $-1<x<1$ B. $-1<x<1$ C. $2<x<4$ D. $2 \le x<4$ E. $-\infty<x<4$

37. $\displaystyle\int_1^2 \dfrac{e^{-1/x}}{x^2}\, dx =$

37____

    A. $e - e^2$ B. $1 - \dfrac{\sqrt{e}}{e}$ C. $\dfrac{\sqrt{e}-1}{e}$ D. $\dfrac{e\sqrt{e}-1}{e}$ E. $\sqrt{e}$

38. $\displaystyle\int_{\pi/4}^{\pi/2} \sin 2x \cos 2x\, d =$

38____

    A. -1 B. $-1/2$ C. $-1/4$ D. $1/4$ E. 1

39. If $y = \ln x$ and n is a positive integer, then $\dfrac{d^n y}{dx^n} =$

39____

    A. $(-1)^{n-1} x^{-n}$ B. $(n-1)x^{n}$ C. $(-1)^{n-1}(n-1)x^{-n}$

    D. $(-1)^{n-1}(n-1)!x^{n}$ E. $(-1)^n n! x^{n}$

40. If at every point of a certain curve the slope of the tangent equals $-2x/y$, the curve is a(n)

40____

A. straight line   B. parabola   C. circle
D. hyperbola   E. ellipse

41. $\int_0^1 \dfrac{dx}{(x^2+1)^{3/2}} =$

A. $\dfrac{1}{2}$ B. $\dfrac{1}{2}\sqrt{2}$ C. 1 D. $\sqrt{2}$ E. $\sin 1$

42. If yz:zx:xy = 1:2:3, then x /yz : y/zx

A. 1:4   B. 1:2   C. 3:2   D. 2:1   E. 4:1

43. Which of the following are horizontal or vertical asymptotes of
3x + 2y + 2 = xy?

I. x = -2/3

II. x = 2

III. y = -1

IV. y = 3

A. None   B. I and III only   C. II and III only
D. II and IV only   E. I,II,III, and IV

44. For what value of b will the line y = 2x + b intersect the parabola $y = x^2$ at right angles?

A. -1   B. -7/16   C. 0   D. 9/16'   E. 3

45. If $y = x^3 - x$, which of the following conditions must be met if y decreases as x increases?

A. $-\dfrac{\sqrt{3}}{3} < x < \dfrac{\sqrt{3}}{3}$ B. $-1/3 < x < 1/3$ C. $x < 1$

D. $-1 < x < 1$ E. $0 < x < 1$

46. $[1 - \dfrac{x}{1!} + \dfrac{x^2}{2!} - \dfrac{x^3}{3!} + ... + \dfrac{(-1)^n x^n}{n!} + ...]e^{2x}dx =$

A. e - 1   B. e   C. e^2 D. $1/3(e^3 - 1)$ E $e^3 - 1$

47. An equation in rectangular coordinates of the curve with polar equation $r^2 = 2r \sec \theta + r \cos \theta$ is

A. $x^2 - x - 2y + y^2 = 0$ B. $x^3 - 3x^2 + xy^2 - 2y^2 = 0$
C. $x^3 - x^2 + xy^2 - 2 = 0$ D. $x^2y - 2x^2 - xy - 2y^2 + y^3 = 0$
E. $x^2y - 2x^2 - 3y2 + y^3 = 0$

48. For what values of y does the pair of equations

$$\begin{cases} x^2 + y^2 - 16 = 0 \\ x^2 - 3y + 12 = 0 \end{cases}$$ have a real solution?

48____

  A. 4only   B. -7,4   C. 0, 4   D. For no y   E. For all y

49. Given that f is a differentiable function on the interval
$0 \leq x \leq 5$ such that $f(0) = 4$ and $f(5) = -1$.

If $g(x) = \dfrac{f(x)}{x+1}$, then there exists some c,

$x + 1$ $0<c<5$, such that $g'(c) =$

49____

  A. -1   B. -5/6   C. -1/6   D. 1/6   E. 5/6

50. The area of the region bounded by a curve with equation y = f(x), the coordinate axes, and the line $x = x_1$ is given by $x_1 e^{x_1}$. Find f(x).

50____

  A. e^x B. xe^x C. $xe^x - e^x$ D. $xe^x + e^x$ E. $x^2 e^x - xe^x$

51. The water in a canal at point P is traveling 10 feet per second, but because of a down-grade its speed is increasing 1/16 foot per second per second. If the rate of increase is constant, how many feet will the water travel from point P in 1 1/15 minutes?

51____

  A. 14   B. 128   C. 644   D. 768   E. 896

52. $f(x) = \dfrac{\cos x}{\dfrac{\pi}{2} - x}$, $x \neq \dfrac{\pi}{2}$, what value MUST be assigned to

$f(\dfrac{\pi}{2})$ in order that f (x) be continuous at $x = \dfrac{\pi}{2}$?

52____

  A. $\dfrac{-\pi}{2}$ B. -1   C. 0   D. 1   E. $\dfrac{\pi}{2}$

53. The function $y = ax^3 + bx^2 + cx + d$ has a point of inflection and a horizontal tangent for the same value of x. What re- lation MUST exist among a, b, and c?

53____

  A. $b = c = 0$ B. $a + b + c = 0$ C. $b^2 - 6ac = 0$
  D. $b^2 - 4ac = 0$ E. $b^2 - 5ac = 0$

54. If $u_{n+1} = iu_{n+1}$, where UT $= i + 1$ and $i = \sqrt{-1}$, find u_{27}.

54____

  A. 0   B. 1   C. i   D. 1 + i   E. 1 - i

55. If the graph of the function g is the reflection in the line y = x of the graph of the function f and if $f(x) = (x+1)^3$, then g(x) =

55____

A. $-(x + 1)^3$ B. $1/(x + 1)^3$ C. $1/(x - 1)^3$
D. $x^{1/3 - 1}$ E. $(x + 1)^{1/3}$

56. What is the mean value of cos 0 over the interval

$0 \leq \theta \leq \dfrac{\pi}{2}$?

A. $\dfrac{1}{2\pi}$ B. $1/2$ C. $\dfrac{2}{\pi}$ D. $\dfrac{\sqrt{2}}{2}$ E. $\dfrac{\pi}{4}$

56____

57. For what value of k does the following system of equations have a solution other than $w = x = y = z = 0$?

$w + x - y + kz = 0$
$w - x - 3y + 2z = 0$
$w + 2x - 2y - 4z = 0$
$w - 3x + 4y + 6z = 0$

A. -2 B. -1 C. 0 D. 2 E. 5

57____

58. Let f be a function symmetric about the Y-axis and de creasing on the interval [1, 3]. Which of the following functions are increasing on [-3, -1]?

I. $-f(x)$

II. $f(-x)$

III. $-f(-x)$

A. I only B. II only C. III only
D. I and II only E. I and III only

58____

59. In how many ways can two brothers and six other boys be seated at a round table so that the brothers are not seated beside each other?

A. 720 B. 1,440 C. 3,600 D. 4,320 E. 5,040

59____

60. Evaluate the double integral $\iint_A xy\,dA$ over the triangle formed by the axes and the line $x + y = 1$.

A. 1/24 B. 1/12 C. 1/8 D. 1/4 E. 1/2

60____

61. If $f(x) = \begin{cases} x & \text{for } x < 1 \\ x-1 & \text{for } x \geq 1, \end{cases}$ then $\displaystyle\int_0^2 x^2 f(x)\,dx =$

A. 1 B. 4/3 C. 5/3 D. 5/2 E. 4

61____

62. Which of the following statements are necessarily true?

I. If a function is differentiable at x, then it is continuous at x.
II. If a function is continuous at x, then it is differentiable at x.
III. If a function is integrable on (x - a, x + a), then it is continuous at x.

A. I only B. II only C. I and II only
D. I and III only E. II and III only

62____

63.

$$\text{If } \sum_{n=5}^{n+5} 4(x-3) \equiv Pn^2 + Qn + R, \text{ then } P + Q =$$

63____

A. 8 B. 10 C. 12 D. 20 E. 24

64.

If $\int_0^{} \int_0^{} e - (x^2 + y^2)\, dx\, dy$ is transformed by the equations

$x = r \cos\theta$, and $y = r \sin\theta$, what is the resultant integral?

64____

A. $\int_0^{} \int_0^{} e^{r^2} dr\, d\theta$

B. $\int_0^{} \int_0^{} e^{-r^2}\, r\, dr\, d\theta$

C. $\int_0^{2\pi} \int_0^{} e^{-r^2}\, r\, dr\, d\theta$

D. $\int_0^{\pi/2} \int_0^{} e^{-r^2}\, r\, dr\, d\theta$

E. $\int_0^{\pi/2} \int_0^{} e^{-r^2}\, r \cos 2\theta\, dr\, d\theta$

65. Find the centroid of the first quadrant area of $x^2 + y^2 = 1$.

65____

A. $\left(\dfrac{\sqrt{2}}{2}, \dfrac{\sqrt{2}}{2}\right)$

B. $\left(\dfrac{4}{3\pi}, \dfrac{4}{3\pi}\right)$

C. $(1/2, 1/2)$

D. $\left(\dfrac{8}{3\pi}, \dfrac{8}{3\pi}\right)$

E. $\left(\dfrac{4}{\pi}, \dfrac{4}{\pi}\right)$

66. Of the following, which is the CLOSEST approximation to the increment of $(x^2 + 7)^{4/5}$ as x increases from 5.0 to 5.1?

66____

A. 0.04 B. 0.08 C. 0.10 D. 0.40 E. 0.80

67. If $d/dx\ g(x) = f(x)$, where $f(x)$ is continuous, then $\int_a^b f(x)g(x)dx =$

67____

A. $f(b) - f(a)$

B. $g(b) - g(a)$

C. $\dfrac{f(b)g(b) - f(a)g(a)}{2}$

D. $\dfrac{[f(b)]^2 - [f(a)]^2}{2}$

E. $\dfrac{[g(b)]^2 - [g(a)]^2}{2}$

68. What is the length from $x = 0$ to $x = \dfrac{\pi}{2}$ of the curve whose slope in this region is given

68____

by $\dfrac{dy}{dx} = \sqrt{\cos^x}$?

A. 1 B. $\sqrt{2}$ C. 3/2 D. 2 E. $3/2\sqrt{2}$

69.

$$\int_{-1}^{1} |\, 2x - 1 \,|\, dx =$$

A. -2   B. 1/2   C. 1 1/2   D. 2   E. 2 1/2

70. If U_n and V_n, n = 1, 2, 3, ..., are sets of real numbers

and if $\sum\limits_{n=1}^{\infty} U_n$ converges, under which of the following con-

ditions is it certain that $\sum\limits_{n=1}^{\infty} V_n$ also converges?

     I. $V_n = 100\, U_{n+5}$, n = 1, 2, 3, ...

     II. $|V_n| < U_n$ for n = 1, 2, 3, ...

     III. $U_n < V_n < 0$ for n= 1, 2, 3, ...

A. I only   B. II only   C. I and II only
D. II and III only   E. I, II, and III

KEY (CORRECT ANSWERS)

1.	D	16.	C	31.	D	46.	A	61.	C
2.	E	17.	E	32.	D	47.	B	62.	A
3.	A	18.	B	33.	B	48.	A	63.	C
4.	B	19.	E	34.	C	49.	B	64.	D
5.	B	20.	B	35.	D	50.	D	65.	B
6.	B	21.	C	36.	C	51.	D	66.	D
7.	C	22.	C	37.	C	52.	D	67.	E
8.	C	23.	E	38.	C	53.	E	68.	D
9.	E	24.	E	39.	D	54.	A	69.	E
10.	A	25.	C	40.	E	55.	D	70.	E
11.	A	26.	C	41.	B	56.	C		
12.	C	27.	A	42.	E	57.	A		
13.	D	28.	D	43.	D	58.	B		
14.	E	29.	D	44.	D	59.	C		
15.	C	30.	E	45.	A	60.	A		

SOLUTIONS TO PROBLEMS

1. Given $y^2 = -2y^3$, $y^2(2y+1) = 0$, so $y = 0$ or $y = -1/2$. Since $y = 1/(x-2)$, $y = 0$ would yield no value for x. But if $y = -1/2$ -, $-1/2 = 1/(x-2)$. Solving, $x = 0$ 1._____

2. From the given equation, $P(e^x+2) + Q(e^x-1) = 2e^x + 3$. This implies that $P + Q = 2$. (Incidentally, $2P - Q = 3$ also.)   2._____

3. Given $x^2 + 2xy + y^2 = 4$, $2x + (2x)(dy/dx) + 2y + (2y)(dy/dx) = 0$. Simplifying, $2x + 2y = -(2x+2y)(dy/dx)$. Thus, $dy/dx = -1$ 3._____

4. $\int x^n \cos x \, dx = x^n \sin x - \int (\sin x)(nx^{n-1})dx$. Thus, $M = nx^{n-1}\sin x$, This illustrates integration by parts, i.e. $\int u\,dv = uv - \int v\,du$, where u and v are functions of x.   4._____

5. Given $y = -4x^4 + px^3 + qx^2 + rx + 5$, $y_1 = 4(1^4) + p(1^3) + q(1^2) + r(-1) + 5 = -p + q - r + q$. Now, $y_1 + y_2 = 2q + 18$ and since it is given that $y_1 + y_2 = 10$, we have $2q + 18 = 10$. Solving, $q = -4$ 5._____

6. Given $f(x) = x - \dfrac{1}{x}$, $f(-x) = -x + \dfrac{1}{x} = -f(x)$. Also, $f(\dfrac{1}{x}) = ,$ 6._____

   $\dfrac{1}{x} - 1/\dfrac{1}{x} = \dfrac{1}{x} - x = -f(x)$. However, note that $f(x^2) =$

   $x^2 - \dfrac{1}{x^2} \neq -f(x) \cdot f(-x)$

7. The equation of the line joining $(0, \dfrac{3}{2})$ and $(\dfrac{9}{4}, 0)$ is   7._____

   $y = -\dfrac{2}{3}x + \dfrac{3}{2}$. If the point $(3, y)$ lies on this line, then $y = (-2/3)(3) + 3/2 = -1/2$

8. If $dx = 3t^2 dt$, then $x = t^3 + c$, where c is a constant. Since $x = 3$ when $t = 1$, $3 = 1^3 + c$, so $c = 2$. Now, $x = t^3 + 2$, and when $t = 2$, $x = 2^3 + 2 = 10$ 8._____

9. Given $f(x) = (x+1)/x$, note that if $g(x) = \dfrac{1}{x-1}$, then ,   9._____

   $f(g(x)) = (\dfrac{1}{x-1} + 1)/(\dfrac{1}{x-1}) = [x/(x-1)] / (\dfrac{1}{x-1}) = x$

10. The tangent to the curve $2x^3 - x^2y^2 + 4y^3 = 16$ has a slope, found by finding dy/dx. Now, $6x^2 - (2x^2y)(dy/dx) - 2xy^2 + (12y^2)(dy/dx) - 0$. At the point $(2,1)$, $24 - 8dy/dx - 4 + 12dy/dx = 0$. Then, $4dy/dx = -20$. Thus, $dy/dx = -5$ 10._____

11. Given $2x + iy - 3y + 2i = 0$, y must be -2. Then, $2x - 3y = 0$. So, $2x - (3)(-2) = 0$, Then, x must be -3. The solution is $x = -3$ and $y = -2$.   11._____

12. $L = ar^{n-1}$ is a geometric sequence where a = 1st term, r = geometric ratio, and L is the nth   12._____
term. Since the 1st and 2nd terms are x^{-4} and x^t, $a = x^{-4}$ and $r = x^t/x^{-4} = x^{t+4}$.
Now, $x^{52} = (x-4)(x^{t+4})^7 = x^{7t+24}$. Thus, 52 = 7t + 24.
Solving, t = 4

13. $y = 1 + e^{-t}$, and since $x = 1 - e^t$, $e^t = 1 - x$, or $e^{-t} = \dfrac{1}{1-x}$. Now, $y = 1 + [1/(1-x)] = (1-x+1)/(1-$ 13._____
x) = (2-x)/(1-x) = (x-2)/(x-1)

14. Given $y = x^3 - 8x + 7$, when x = 3, y = 10, and t = 0 dy/dx $= 3x^2 - 8$, so dy/dx at x = 3 = 19.   14._____
Now, dy/dt = (dy/dx)(dx/dt). Since dx/dt at t = 0 is 2, we have dy/dt = (19)(2) = 38

15. Let x = number of weeks. If y = amount of yield for x weeks, then y = (100+10x)(1.50-   15._____
.05x) = 150 + 10x - $.5x^2$. To maximize y, set dy/dx = 0. dy/dx = 10 - x = 0, so x = 10
(Note: The maximum y = $200)

16. $2t^3 - 3t^2 < 0$ can be written as $(t^2)(2t-3) < 0$. This implies either $t^2 < 0$ and 2t - 3 > 0 or the   16._____
condition that $t^2 > 0$ and 2t - 3 < 0. Since t must be at least 0, the first of these
two conditions is impossible. Solving, $t^2 > 0$ and 2t - 3 < 0
yields 0 < t < 3/2

17. $V = \pi r^2 h$ for a cylinder. Differentiating with respect to time   17._____

(t), $dV/dt = (\pi r^2)(dh/dt) + 2\pi rh(dr/dt) = (\pi)(16)(1/8) + (2\pi)(4)(6)(\dfrac{1}{2}) = 26\pi$ cu· in· per

min.

18. To find $\lim\limits_{t \to \infty} t^3 e^{-t}$, use L'Hôspital's rule ·   18._____

$\lim\limits_{t \to \infty} t^3 e^{-t} = \lim\limits_{t \to \infty}(t^3/e^t) = \lim\limits_{t \to \infty}(3t^2/e^t)$

$= \lim\limits_{t \to \infty}(6t/e^t) = \lim\limits_{t \to \infty}(6/e^t) = 0$

19. F(2) = 2F(0) - F(I) = 1. F(3) = 2F(1) - F(2) - 5 F(4) = 2F(2) - F(3) = -3. Finally, F(5) = 2F(3)   19._____
- F(4) = 10 - (-3) = 13

20. If $x = t^3 - 4$ and $y = 2t^2 + 1$, then $y = 2(x+4)2/3 + 1$. At t = 2, x = 4, and y = 9. Now, dy/dx =   20._____

$(2)(2/3)(x+4)^{-\frac{1}{3}} = 4/3(x+4)^{-\frac{1}{3}}$. At (4, 9), dy/dx = 2/3. The tangent to the curve y

$2(x+4)^{-\frac{2}{3}}$· contains the point (4,9) and has a slope of 2/3 The equation of the tangent

can be written as $y = \dfrac{2}{3}x + \dfrac{19}{3}$ or 2x - 3y + 19 = 0

21. ____

21. $e^{-x} = 1 - x + \dfrac{x^2}{2!} - \dfrac{x^3}{3!} + \ldots$ Let $f(x) = e^{-x}$ so that $f'(x) = -e^{-x}$, $f''(x) = e^{-x}$ and $f'''(x) = -e^{-x}$.

By the MacLaurin Series, $f(x) = f(0) + p'(0)x + f''(0)x^2/2! + f'''(0)x^3/3! + \ldots$ For $x = 1/5$, $f(1/5)$

$= 1 - (1)(+1/5) + (1/25)/2 - (1)(+\dfrac{1}{125})/6 \approx .82$

22. ____

22. $\dfrac{\partial^2 \phi}{\partial x \partial y} = \dfrac{\partial}{\partial x}(\dfrac{\partial \phi}{\partial y}) = \dfrac{\partial}{\partial x}(-x \sin y) = -\sin y$

$\dfrac{\partial^2 \phi}{\partial z^2} = \dfrac{\partial}{\partial z}(\dfrac{\partial \phi}{\partial z}) = \dfrac{\partial}{\partial z}(x \sec^2 z) = 2x \sec^2 z \, \tan z$

$\dfrac{\partial^2 \phi}{\partial y \partial z} = \dfrac{\partial}{\partial y}(\dfrac{\partial \phi}{\partial z}) = \dfrac{\partial}{\partial y}(x \sec^2 z) = 0$

23. ____

23. $\text{Log}_8 m + \text{Log}_8 \dfrac{1}{6} = \text{Log}_8 \dfrac{1}{6} m = \dfrac{2}{3}$. Then, $\dfrac{1}{6}m = 8^{\frac{2}{3}} = 4$ Solving, $m = 24$

24. ____

24. The slope of $y = -x^3 + 3x^2 + 9x - 27$ is given by $dy/dx = -3x^2 + 6x + 9$. To maximize the slope set $d^2y/dx^2 = 0$. $d^2y/dx^2 = -6x + 6 = 0$, yielding $x = 1$. At $x = 1$, $dy/dx = -3(1^2) + (6)(1) + 9 = 12$

25. ____

25. For the expression $(x - mx^{-1})^{11}$, the 1st term is x^{11}, the 2nd term is $-(11x^{10})(mx^{-1}) = -11mx^9$, the 3rd term would be $+ [(11)(10)/2!](x^9)(mx^{-1})^2 = +55m^2 x^7$. By this pattern, the 8th term would contain x^{-3}. The 8th term would be $- [(11)(10)(\ldots)(5)/7!](x^4)(mx^{-1})^7 = -330m^7 x^{-3}$, so the coefficient of x^{-3} is $-300m^7$.

26. ____

26. Given $y^2 + 6x = 36$, then $y = \pm\sqrt{36 - 6x}$. In the 1st quadrant, the vertices of the enclosed area are $(0,6)$, $(0,0)$, $(6,0)$.. The required volume is given by

$\int_0^6 (\sqrt{36 - 6x})^2 \cdot \pi \, dx \quad \int_0^6 (36\pi - 6\pi x) \, dx = [36\pi x - 3\pi x^2]_0^6 = 216\pi - 108\pi = 108\pi$

27. ____

27. Total area bounded by $y = x^2$, x-axis, and $x = 2^{\frac{1}{3}} = \int_0^{2^{\frac{1}{3}}} x^2 dx = [x^3/3]_0^{2^{\frac{1}{3}}} = \dfrac{2}{3}$. To find k such that area bounded by $y = x^2$, x-axis, and $x = k$ is $1/3$, we

have $\int_0^k x^2 dx = [x^3/3]_0^k = K^3/3 = \dfrac{1}{3}$ Then, $k = 1$

28. ____

28. $\text{Lim}_{x \to 0}[2\tan^2 x / (1 - \cos^2 x)] = \text{Lim}_{x \to 0}[2\tan^2 x / \sin^2 x] = \text{Lim}_{x \to 0} 2\sec^2 x = 2$

29. ____

29. Since the parabola contains $(4, 4)$ with vertex at $(0, 0)$, its equation must be of the form $y = kx^2$, where k is a constant. Then, $4 = (k)(4^2)$, so $k = 1/4$. Equation becomes $y = 1/4x^2$, and for $x = 6$, $y = (1/4)(6^2) = 9$

30. To be a pair of straight lines, $4x^2 + 8xy + ky^2$ must be a perfect trinomial square. This means k = 4, since $4x^2 + 8xy + 4y^2 = (2x+2y)^2$. The equation becomes $(2x+2y)^2 = 9$, which implies 2x + 2y = 3 and 2x + 2y = -3

30._____

31. The midpoint of the line segment joining (1, 5) and (-3, 2) is (-1, 3 1/2) and the slope of this segment is (5-2)/(1+3) = 3/4. The perpendicular bisector must contain (-1, 3 1/2) and have slope of - 4/3. Then, y = - 4/3x + b would represent the required equation. Substituting (-1,3 1/2), 3-1/2 = (-4/3)(-1) + b, so b = 13/6 . Now, we get $y = -\dfrac{4}{3}x + \dfrac{13}{6}$, which becomes 8x + 6y - 13 = 0

31._____

32. dy/dx = $[(1+ex)(-x \sin x + \cos x) - (e^x)(x \cos x)]/(1+e^x)^2$. At x = 0, dy/dx = $[(2)(1)-(1)(0)]/4$ = 1/2

32._____

33. $(1-\dfrac{1}{4})(1-\dfrac{1}{5})(1-\dfrac{1}{6})(...)(1-\dfrac{1}{n+2})(1-\dfrac{1}{n+3}) = (\dfrac{3}{4})(\dfrac{4}{5})(\dfrac{5}{6})(...) \cdot (\dfrac{n+1}{n+2})(\dfrac{n+2}{n+3}) = \dfrac{3}{n+3}$

33._____

34. $1+i = \sqrt{2}(\cos 45° + i \sin 45°)$. By De Moivre's Theorem,

$[\sqrt{2} \cos 45°]^9 = (\sqrt{2})^9 [\cos(9 \cdot 45)°] = + i \sin(9.45)] = 16\sqrt{2}[\dfrac{\sqrt{2}}{2} + i\dfrac{\sqrt{2}}{2}] = 16 + 16i$

34._____

35. Since $\log_5 k = \dfrac{1}{\log_k 5}$, $\log_k x \cdot \log_5 k = \log_k x \div \log_k 5 = 3$. This implies that x = 5^3 = 125

35._____

36. Given $1 + 2(x-3) + 3(x-3)^2 + 4(x-3)^3 + ...$, we need to find $\lim\limits_{n \to \infty} |u_{n+1} / u_n|$, where $u_n + i$ and u_n represent the $(n + 1)^{st}$- and nth terms. =

$\lim\limits_{n \to \infty} |u_{n+1} / u_n| = \lim\limits_{n \to \infty} |(n+1)(x-3)^n / (n)(x-3)^{n-1}| = x - 3$. This series will converge if |x-3| < 1, which implies 2 < x < 4

36._____

37. If $u = e^{-\frac{1}{x}}$, $du = (e^{-\frac{1}{x}})(\dfrac{1}{x^2})dx$. Thus, $\int_1^2 (e^{-\frac{1}{x}})(\dfrac{1}{x^2})dx = [e^{-\frac{1}{x}}]_1^2 = e^{-\frac{1}{2}} - e^{-1} = \dfrac{1}{\sqrt{e}} - \dfrac{1}{e} = \dfrac{\sqrt{e}-1}{e}$

37._____

38. $\int_{\pi/4}^{\pi/2} \sin 2x \cos 2x \, dx = \dfrac{1}{2}\int_{\pi/4}^{\pi/2} \sin 2x \cdot \cos 2x \, dx = [\dfrac{(\sin 2x)^2}{4}]_{\pi/4}^{\pi/2} = \dfrac{0^2}{4} - \dfrac{1^2}{4} = -\dfrac{1}{4}$

38._____

39. Given $y = Lnx$, $dy/dx = \dfrac{1}{x}$, $d^2y/dx^2 = -\dfrac{1}{x^2}$, $d^3y/dx^3 = -\dfrac{2!}{x^3}$, $d^4y/dx^4 = -3!/x^4$. In general, we have

$d^ny/dx^n = [(-1)^{n-1}][(n-1)!x^n] = [(-1)^{n-1}][(n-1)!x^n]$

39._____

40. The slope of the tangent = dy/dx = -2x/y. This means ydy = -2xdx, which leads to $y^2/2 = -x^2 + k$, where k is a constant. This is equivalent to $2x^2 + y^2 = C$, where C = another constant. This equation represents an ellipse.

40._____

41. $\int_0^1 dx / (x^2+1)^{\frac{3}{2}}$ can be evaluated by letting $x = \tan u$, so $dx = \sec^2 u\, du$. The integral can

then be written as $\int_0^1 \sec^2 u\, du /(\tan^2 u+1)^{\frac{3}{2}} = \int_0^1 \sec^2 du /(\sec^2 u)^{\frac{3}{2}} =$

$\int_0^1 du/\sec u = [\sin u]_0^1 = [x / \sqrt{x^2+1}]_0^1 = \dfrac{1}{\sqrt{2}} = \dfrac{1}{2}\sqrt{2}$

41.____

42. Since yz:zx = 1:2, x = 2y. (Also, 2x:xy = 2:3, 2y = 3z). x/yz = 2y/yz = 2/z and y/zx = y/
(2)(2y) .= 1/2z. Now, x/yz:y/zx = 2/z:1/2z = (2/z)-(2z/1) = 4:1

42.____

43. An asymptote of a curve must contain no points of that curve. If x = - 2/3, -2 + 2y + 2 = -
2/3y, so y = 0. If x = 2, 6 + 2y + 2 = 2y, so there is no solution for y. If y = -1, 3x - 2 + 2 = -
x, so x = 0. If y = 3, 3x + 6 + 2 = 3x, so there is no solution for x. The asymptotes are x =
2 and y = 3

43.____

44. The slope of y = 2x + b is 2. At the point of intersection with $y = x^2$ at right angles, the
slope of $y = x^2$ must be -1/2. Since the slope of $y = x^2$ is 2x, let 2x = 1/2, so x = -1/4.
Then, $y = (-1/4)^2 = 1/16$ Now, (-1/4,1/16) must lie on y = 2x + b. Substituting, 1/16 = 2(-1/
4) + b, so b = 9/16

44.____

45. Given $y = x^3-x$, the interval in which y decreases as x increases coincides with dy/dx < 0.
Now, $dy/dx = 3x^2-1$, so $3x^2-1 <0$ implies $-\sqrt{1/3} < x < \sqrt{1/3}$. This is equivalent to

$-\sqrt{3/3} < x < \sqrt{3/3}$

45.____

46. since $e^{-x} =1 -x/1! + x^2/2! - + x^3/3! + ...$, the given integral

becomes $\int_0^1 e^{-x} e^{2x}\, dx = \int_0^1 e^x dx = [e^x]_0^1 = e -1$

46.____

47. $r = \sqrt{x^2 + y^2}, \sec\theta = \dfrac{r}{x}, \cos\theta = \dfrac{x}{r}$. Thus, $r^2 = 2r\sec\theta + r\cos\theta$

becomes $x^2 + y^2 = (2)(\sqrt{x^2+y^2})(\sqrt{x^2+y^2}/x) + (\sqrt{x^2+y^2})(x/\sqrt{x^2+y^2})$

Simplifying, we get $x^2 + y^2 = 2/x\,(x^2+y^2) + x$. Multiplying by x and putting all terms on
the left side of the equation, $x^3 - 3x^2 +xy^2 - 2y^2 = 0$

47.____

48. Subtracting the second equation from the first equation, we get $y^2 + 3y - 28 = 0$. Factor-
ing, (y+7)(y-4) = 0, which yields y = -7 and y = 4. If y = 4, x = 0. But substituting y = -7
leads to $x^2 = -33$ for which there is no real solution. So only y = 4 gives a real solution
ordered pair.

48.____

49. g(0) = f(0)/(0+1) = 4 and g(5) = f(5)/(5+1) = - 1/6 . Since f(x) is differentiable (and also
continuous) on [0,5], so is g(x) on this interval. By the Mean Value Theorem, there must
exist c, 0 < c < 5, such that g'(c) equals the slope of the line connecting (0,4) and (5,- 1/
6), which is [4-(- 1/6)]/[0-5] = - 5/6

49.____

50. $x_1 e^{x_1} = \int_0^{x_1} f(x)\, dx$. Let $F(x) = \int f(x)\, dx$. Then, $f(x_1) - F(0) = x_1 e^{x_1}$, $x_1 e^{x_1}$,

Which imlpies $F(x) = x e^x$. So, $f(x) = F'(x) = (d/dx)(x e^x) = x e^x + e^x$

50.____

51. The distances in each of the first 3 seconds are 10 1/16 ft. 10 2/16 ft., and 10 3/16 ft. In the 64th second (1 1/15 min), the distance is $10 + (64)(1/16) = 14$ ft. The total distance traveled = 10 1/16 + 10 2/16 + 14. Since this is an arithmetic series, the sum is $(64/2)(10\ 1/16 + 14) = 770$ ft.

51.____

52. $f(x) = \cos x / (\frac{\pi}{2} - x)$, $x \neq \frac{\pi}{2}$. In order for $f(x)$ to be continuous at $x = \frac{\pi}{2}$,

$f = (\frac{\pi}{2})$ must equal $\lim\limits_{x \to \frac{\pi}{2}} [\cos x / (\frac{\pi}{2} - x)]$. Using L'Hôpital's

Rule, this limit equals $\lim\limits_{x \to \frac{\pi}{2}} - \sin x / -1 = 1$. So, $f('o\,')$ must equal 1

52.____

53. At a point of inflection, the 2nd derivative $(d^2y/dx^2) = 0$, and for a horizontal tangent, the 1st derivative $(dy/dx) = 0$. Given $y = ax^3 + bx^2 + cx + d$, $dy/dx = 3ax^2 + 2bx + c = 0$ and $d^2y/dx^2 = 6ax + 2b = 0$. From the 2nd equation, $x = -b/3a$. Substituting into the 1st equation, $3a(-b/3a)^2 + 2b(-b/3a) + c = 0$. Then, $b^2/3a - 2b^2/3a + c = 0$, and this will simplify to $b^2 - 3ac = 0$

53.____

54. $u_1 = i + 1$, $u_2 = iu_1 + 1 = i(i+1) + 1 = i^2 + i + 1$. In general, $u_k = i^k + i^{k-1} + i^{k-2} + \dots + i + 1$. Thus, $u^{27} = i^{27} + i^{26} + \dots i + 1$. Note that $1 + i + i^2 + i^3 = 0$, $i^4 + i^5 + i^6 + i^7 = 0, \dots, i^{24} + i^{25} + i^{26} + i^{27} = o$. Thus, $u^{27} = 0$

54.____

55. $g(x)$ must be $f^{-1}(x)$, since it is the reflection of $f(x)$ about the line $y = x$. Now, $f(x) = (x+1)^3$, so $f{-1}(x) = g(x) = \sqrt[3]{x} - 1$ or $x^{\frac{1}{3}} - 1$

55.____

56. Mean value of $\cos\theta = [\int_0^{\pi/2} \cos\theta\, d\theta] / [\frac{\pi}{2} - 0] = [\sin\theta]_0^{\pi/2} \div \frac{\pi}{2}$

$= (\sin\frac{\pi}{2} - \sin\theta) / \frac{\pi}{2} = \frac{2}{\pi}$

56.____

57. In order to have a solution set different from $w = x = y = z = 0$, one coefficient of 2 variables must be a multiple of another coefficient of 2 variables. Subtracting equation 2 from equation 1, we get $2x + 2y + (k-2)z = 0$ (call it equation A). Subtracting equation 3 from equation 2, we get $-3x + y + 6z = 0$ (call it equation B). Doubling equation B and subtracting from equation A, $8x + (k-14)z = 0$. For integral solutions, $k - 14$ must be a multiple of 8. For positive k values, $k = 6, 14, 22, 30, \dots$ and for negative k values, $k = -2, -10, -18, -26, \dots$ Among the five choices is $k = -2$. The solutions become $w = 0$, $y = 0$, and $x = 2z (x, z \neq 0)$. Example: $w = 0$, $x = 4$, $y = 0$, $z = 2$.

57.____

58. Since f(x) is symmetric about the y-axis, f(-x) must equal f(x). If f(x) is decreasing on [1,3], then f(-x) must be increasing on [-3,-1]. Note: -f(x) and -f(-x) do not necessarily increase on [-3,-1].

58.____

59. Assign the first brother to any seat. In order for the second brother to sit in a non-adjacent seat, there are 5 available seats. For each of these 5 seat selections, there are 6! = 720 ways of seating the other 6 boys. The total number of seating arrangements is (720)(5) = 3600.

59.____

60. $\iint_A xy\,dA = \int_0^1 [\int_0^{1-y} xy\,dx]\,dy = \int_0^1 \frac{x^2 y}{2}\Big|_0^{1-y}\,dy = \int_0^1 \frac{y(1-y)^2}{2}\,dy =$

$\frac{1}{2}\int_0^1 (y-2y^2+y^3)\,dy = \frac{1}{2}[\frac{y^2}{2} - \frac{2y^3}{3} + \frac{y^4}{4}]_0^1 = \frac{1}{2}[\frac{1}{2} - \frac{2}{3} + \frac{1}{4}] = \frac{1}{24}$

60.____

61. $\int_0^2 x^2 f(x)\,dx = \int_0^1 x^2\,dx + \int_1^2 x^2(x-1)\,dx = [\frac{x^4}{4}]_0^1 + [\frac{x^4}{4} - \frac{x^3}{3}]_1^2$

=1/4 + 17/12 + 5/3

61.____

62. If a function is differentiable at x, it is always continuous at x, but not necessarily vice-versa. Also, a function may be integrable on an open interval and not necessarily continuous at each point of that interval. To be integrable, there must be at most a finite number of discontinuities.

62.____

63. $\sum_{n-5}^{n+5} (4(x-3)) = 8 + 12 + 16 + \ldots + (4n + 8)$. This is an x = 5 arithmetic series with 1st term = 8, last term = 4n+8, and n+1 terms. Sum = n+1/2[8+(4n+8)] = $2n^2 + 10n + 8$. If $2n^2 + 10n + 8 = Pn^2 + Qn + R$, then P = 2, Q = 10, R = 8. So, P + Q = 12

63.____

64. The mass of this 1st quadrant $= m = \frac{1}{4}\pi(1^2) = \frac{\pi}{4}$.

64.____

The x-moment $Mx = \int_0^1 \frac{1}{2} f(x)\,dx = \int_0^1 \frac{1}{2}(1-x^2)\,dx = [\frac{1}{2}x - \frac{1}{6}x^3]_0^1 = \frac{1}{3}$

The y-moment $My = \int_0^1 x \cdot f(x)\,dx = \int_0^1 x \cdot \sqrt{1-x^2}\,dx = [-\frac{1}{3}(1-x^2)^{\frac{3}{2}}]_0^1 = \frac{1}{3}$.

The centroid is given by $(\bar{x},\bar{y})$, Where $\bar{x} = \frac{My}{m} = \frac{1}{3}/\frac{\pi}{4} = \frac{4}{3\pi}$

and $\bar{y} = Mx/m = \frac{1}{3}/\frac{p}{4} = \frac{4}{3\pi}$. Thus, $(\bar{x},\bar{y}) = (\frac{4}{3\pi}, \frac{4}{3\pi})\times$

65. If x = 5.0, $(x^2+7)^{\frac{4}{5}} \approx 16.40$. If x = 5.0, $(x^2+7)^{\frac{4}{5}} \approx 16.40$. The resulting increment is about .40.

65.____

66. $\int_a^b f(x) \cdot g(x)\,dx = \int_a^b (\frac{d}{dx} g(x) \cdot g(x)\,dx] = [\frac{(g(x))^2}{2}]_a^b = \{[g(b)]^2 - [y(a)]^2\}/2$

66.____

67.____

67. For any y = f(x), the length of the curve from x = 0 to $x = \dfrac{\pi}{2}$ is given by

$\int_0^{\pi/2} \sqrt{1+[f'(x)]^2}\ dx$ · Here, $dy/dx = f'(x) = (\cos x)^{\frac{1}{2}}$,

so we get $\int_0^{\pi/2} \sqrt{1+\cos x}\ dx$. since $\cos \dfrac{1}{2}x = \sqrt{1+\cos x}/\sqrt{2}$, the integral

becomes $\sqrt{2} \int_0^{\pi/2} \cos \dfrac{1}{2}x\ dx = [2\sqrt{2}\sin\dfrac{1}{2}x]_0^{\pi/2} = 2\sqrt{2}(\sin \dfrac{\pi}{4} - \sin 0) = 2$

68.____

68. $\int_{-1}^{1} |2x-1|\ dx = \int_{-1}^{\frac{1}{2}} (1-2x)\ dx + \int_{\frac{1}{2}}^{1} (2x-1)\ dx = [x-x^2]_{-1}^{\frac{1}{2}} + [x^2-x]_{\frac{1}{2}}^{1} =$

$1/4 + 2 + 0 + 1/4 = 2\ 1/2$

69.____

69. $\sum_{n=1}^{\prime} V_n$ will converge if each term of V_n is a multiple of all n=i but a finite number of terms of U_n or if $|V_n| < U_n$ for all n. Also, note that if $U_n < V_n < 0$, then $|V_n| < |U_n|$ and will also converge.

EXAMINATION SECTION
TEST 1

DIRECTIONS: Each question or incomplete statement is followed by several suggested answers or completions. Select the one that BEST answers the question or completes the statement.

Questions 1-2.

DIRECTIONS: Questions 1 and 2 are based on Table I, which appears immediately below.

Table I

x	u_x	Δ	Δ^2	Δ^3	Δ^4
0	1				
		2			
1	3		4		
		6		-3	
2	9		1		-2
		7		-5	
3	16		-4		
		3			
4	19				

Assume fourth differences are constant.

1.   Using Table I, determine the numerical value of $\mu\delta^3 u_1$.

    A.   -8
    B.   -6
    C.   -5
    D.   -4
    E.   -2
    F.   0
    G.   7
    H.   Cannot be determined from data given.

2.   Using Table I, determine the numerical value of

$(1-\frac{\Delta}{E})^{-1}_{u_3}$

    A.   4
    B.   6
    C.   8
    D.   9
    E.   16
    F.   19
    G.   21
    H.   23

3. Evaluate $\sum\limits_{x=0}^{9} (x+3)(x+4)(x+5)$.

   $x = 0$
   A. 1360
   B. 5976
   C. 8100
   D. 8160
   E. 8190
   F. 10,830
   G. 32,400
   H. 32,640

4. Which one of the following polynomials has $12x^2 - 6x$ as its second ordinary advancing difference?
   A. $x^4 - 5x^3 + 8x^2 + 1$
   B. $x^4 - 5x^3 + 4x - 1$
   C. $x^4 - x^3 + x$
   D. x^4
   E. 24
   F. $x^4 + 7x^3 + 10^{x2} + 2x$
   G. $4x^3 + 3x^2 + 2x - 3$
   H. None of the above

5. If $u_x = x^4 + 2x^3 + 3x^2 + 2x + 1$, then

   $\Delta^3_{bcd}\, u_a - \Delta^3_{bce}\, u_a = (?)$
   A. 0
   B. $e - d$
   C. $d - e$
   D. $\dfrac{d-e}{4}$
   E. $\dfrac{d-e}{4!}$ $\Delta^4_{bcde}\, u_a$
   F. $4(a - 6)$
   G. $d + e - 2a$
   H. $(e - a) + (d - a)\, \Delta^3_{bce}\, (u_d - u_a)$

6. If $u_x = 1 + (x-a) + \dfrac{(x-a)(x-b)}{2}$

   $\dfrac{(x-a)(x-b)(x-c)}{4} + \dfrac{(x-a)(x-b)(x-c)(x-d)}{8}$, then $\Delta^2_{bc}\, u_a = (?)$

A. $\dfrac{1}{8}$

B. $\dfrac{1}{4}$

C. $\dfrac{1}{2}$

D. 1

E. $\dfrac{2a^2}{(a-b)(a-c)(b-c)}$

F. $\dfrac{2(bc+ac+ab)}{(a-b)(a-c)(b-c)}$

G. $\dfrac{c-b+2}{2}$

H. $\dfrac{2(c-a)+c^2-(a+b)c+ab}{2(c-a)}$

7. If $\Delta^4 u_x = 0$ for all values of x, and $u_0 = 16$, $u_1 = 32$, $u_2 = 10$, $u_3 = 22$, and $u_4 = 140$, find

$\int_0^4 u_x\,dx.$

   A. 196/3
   B. 80
   C. 382/3
   D. 392/3
   E. 158
   F. 220
   G. 658
   H. 5576/3

8. If x, y, z are uncorrelated statistical variables with standard deviations 5, 12, 9, respectively, and if $u = x + y$ and $v = y + z$, find the correlation coefficient r between u and v.
   A. 0
   B. 13/270
   C. 4/65
   D. 13/135
   E. 58/441
   F. 48/119
   G. 1/2
   H. 48/65

9. What is the probability of throwing exactly 9 heads exactly twice in 5 throws of 10 true coins?

A. $\left(\dfrac{50!}{41!\,9!}\right)^2 \left(\dfrac{1}{2}\right)^{100}$

B. $\dfrac{50!}{18!\,32!}\left(\dfrac{1}{2}\right)^{50}$

C. $10\left(\dfrac{1}{11}\right)^2 \left(\dfrac{10}{11}\right)^3$

D. $10\left(\dfrac{1}{2^9}\right)^2 \left(1-\dfrac{1}{2^9}\right)^3$

E. $10\left(\dfrac{10}{2^{10}}\right)^2 \left(1-\dfrac{10}{2^{10}}\right)^3$

F. $\dfrac{50!}{9!\,41!}\left(\dfrac{1}{2}\right)^{50}$

G. $\dfrac{1}{2^9}$

H. $10\left(\dfrac{10}{2^{10}}\right)^3 \left(1-\dfrac{10}{2^{10}}\right)^2$

10. Two samples of 100 cases each have variances 14 and 18, respectively. The square of the difference between the means of the two samples is 20. If the two samples are pooled to form a single sample of 200 cases, what is the variance of the pooled sample?
   A. 12
   B. 16
   C. 21
   D. 26
   E. 30
   F. 32
   G. 35
   H. 36

11. The means and standard deviations of scores obtained by administering tests T and R to a group of students are as follows:

	Mean	σ
Test T	75	18
Test R	40	6

The correlation between tests T and R is 0.75. Student K made a score of 103 on test T but did not take test R. What is the best estimate which can be made of the score which student K would have obtained on Test R, if he had taken it?

A. 40
B. 47
C. 49
D. 55
E. 61
F. 63
G. 68
H. 103

12. *M* throws 3 coins and *N* rolls 2 dice. If this experiment is repeated 10 times, what is the probability that 3 heads and a pair of sixes appear simultaneously at least once?

A. $\dfrac{1}{288}$

B. $\dfrac{5}{144}$

C. $1-\left(\dfrac{143}{144}\right)^{10}$

D. $1-\left(\dfrac{245}{288}\right)^{10}$

E. $1-\left(\dfrac{287}{288}\right)^{10}$

F. $\dfrac{287}{288}$

G. $\left(\dfrac{287}{288}\right)^{9}$

H. $\sum\limits_{i=1}^{9}\left(\dfrac{287}{288}\right)^{i}$

13. Let the proportions of families in a given state having 0, 1, 2, 3, ... children be p_0, p_1, p_2, p_3, ... $(\sum p_4 = 1)$. Estimate the proportion of all families having exactly j sons. (Assume that the probability of having sons or daughters is equal.)

A. $\sum\limits_{i \geq j} \dfrac{\binom{i}{j}}{2^i} p_i$

B. $\sum\limits_{i \geq j} \dfrac{1}{2^i} p_i$

C. $\dfrac{1}{2} \sum\limits_{i \geq j} \binom{i}{j} p_i$

D. $\sum\limits_{i \geq j} \dfrac{\binom{i}{j}}{2^j}$

E. $\sum\limits_{i \geqslant j} \dfrac{\binom{i}{j}}{2^j} P_i$

F. $\sum\limits_{i \geqslant j} \dfrac{\binom{i}{j}}{2^i}$

G. $\sum\limits_{i \geqslant j} \dfrac{P_i}{2^i}$

H. $\sum\limits_{i \geqslant j} \dfrac{1}{2^i}$

14.   A lot contains n articles. If it is known that r of the articles are defective, and the articles are inspected in a random order, one at a time, what is the probability that the kth article inspected will be the last defective one in the lot?

A. $\binom{k}{r}\left(\dfrac{r}{n}\right)^r\left(\dfrac{n-r}{n}\right)^{k-r}$

B. $\dfrac{1}{\binom{n}{r}}$

C. $\dfrac{\binom{n-r}{n-k}\binom{k-1}{r-1}}{n!}$

D. $\dfrac{\binom{k-1}{r-1}}{\binom{n}{r}}$

E. $\dfrac{\binom{k}{r}}{\binom{n}{r}}$

F. $\dfrac{\binom{r}{r-1}\binom{n-r}{n-k}}{\binom{m}{k-1}}$

G. $\dfrac{\binom{r}{r-1}\binom{n-k}{n-r}}{\binom{n}{k-1}}$

H. $\dfrac{1}{n-k+1}$

15. Extensive tests show that 80% of a certain kind of grass seed germinates. If a sample of 900 seeds is taken from a sack of this grass seed, the probability is approximately .9773 that at least how many of the seeds will germinate?

    A. 684
    B. 696
    C. 700
    D. 704
    E. 708
    F. 720
    G. 744
    H. 880

KEY (CORRECT ANSWERS)

1.	E		6.	C
2.	F		7.	D
3.	D		8.	H
4.	A		9.	E
5.	C		10.	C

11.	B
12.	E
13.	A
14.	D
15.	B

EXAMINATION SECTION
TEST 1

DIRECTIONS: Each question or incomplete statement is followed by several suggested answers or completions. Select the one that BEST answers the question or completes the statement.

The reference tables needed for solving the problems and notes concerning definitions and conventions used in the examination are set forth below on pages 1-5.

REFERENCE TABLES AND NOTES (Pages 1-5)

NOTE.- Throughout this examination, $Pr(E)$ is the probability that the event E occurs.

$\binom{n}{r}$ is the number of combinations of n objects taken r at a time.

ln x is the natural logarithm of x.

All problems involving cards refer to an ordinary deck of 52 playing cards consisting of 4 suits of 13 cards each. A bridge hand consists of 13 cards.

Unless otherwise specified, all problems involving dice refer to the ordinary six-sided die.

If A and B are sets, then $A \cup B$ (the union of A and B) is the set of all elements belonging either to A or to B; $A \cap B$ (the intersection of A and B) is the set of all elements belonging both to A and to B.

Normal Distribution

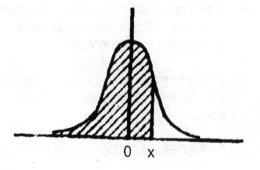

The tables below give the value of dt for certain values of

$$F(x) = \frac{1}{\sqrt{2p}} \int_{-\infty}^{x} e^{-t^{2/2}} \, d\,t \text{ for certain values oe x.}$$

x	.0	.1	.2	3	.4	.5	.6	.7	.8	.9
0	.5000	5398	.5793	.6179	.6554	6915	.7257	.7580	7881	.8159
1	.8413	8643	.88-19	9032	9192	9332	.9452	.9554	.9641	.9713
2	.9772	.9821	.9861	.9893	9918	.9938	.9953	.9965	.9974	.9981
3	.9987	9990	.9993	.9995	.9997					

x	1.282	1 440	1.645	1.960	2.326	2.576	3.090
F(x)	0.900	0.925	0.950	0.975	0.990	0.995	0.999

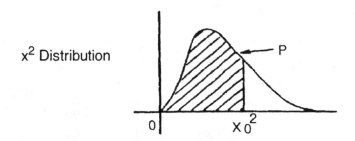

x^2 Distribution

For a given number of degrees of freedom and a given value of P, the table below gives the value Xo^2 for which $Pr(x^2 < Xo^2) = P$

Degrees of freedom	Value of P							
	0.005	0.010	0.025	0.050	0.950	0.975	0.990	0.995
1	0.000	0.000	0.001	0.004	3.84	5.02	6.63	7.88
2	0.010	0.020	0.051	0.103	5.99	7.38	9.21	10.6
3	0.072	0.115	0.216	0.352	7.81	9.35	11.3	12.8
4	0.207	0.297	0.484	0.711	9.49	11.1	13.3	14.9
5	0.412	0.554	0.831	1.15	11.1	12.8	15.1	16.7
6	0.676	0.872	1.24	1.64	12.6	14.4	16.8	18.5
7	0.989	1.24	1.69	2.17	14.1	16.0	18.5	20.3
8	1.34	1.65	2.18	2.73	15.5	17.5	20.1	22.0
9	1.73	2.09	2.70	3.33	16.9	19.0	21.7	23.6
10	2.16	2.56	3.25	3.94	18.3	20.5	23.2	25.2
11	2.60	3.05	3.82	4.57	19.7	21.9	24.7	26.8
12	3.07	3.57	4.40	5.23	21.0	23.3	26.2	28.3
13	3.57	4.11	5.01	5.89	22.4	24.7	27.7	29.8
14	4.07	4.66	5.63	6.57	23.7	26.1	29.1	31.3
15	4.60	5.23	6.26	7.26	25.0	27.5	30.6	32.8
16	5.14	5.81	6.91	7.96	26.3	28.8	32.0	34.3
17	5.70	6.41	7.56	8.67	27.6	30.2	33.4	35.7
18	6.26	7.01	8.23	9.39	28.9	31.5	34.8	37.2
19	6.84	7.63	8.91	10.1	30.1	32.9	36.2	38.6
20	7.43	8.26	9.59	10.9	31.4	34.2	37.6	40.0

For a given number of degrees of freedom and a given value of P, the table below gives the value t_0 for which $Pr(-\infty < l < t_o) = P$.

Degrees of freedom	Value of P				
	0.900	0.950	0.975	0.990	0.995
1	3.08	6.31	12.7	31.8	63.7
2	1.89	2.92	4.30	6.96	9.92
3	1.64	2.35	3.18	4.54	5.84
4	1.53	2.13	2.78	3.75	4.60
5	1.48	2.02	2.57	3.36	4.03
6	1.44	1.94	2.45	3.14	3.71
7	1.42	1.90	2.36	3.00	3.50
8	1.40	1.86	2.31	2.90	3.36
9	1.38	1.83	2.26	2.82	3.25
10	1.37	1.81	2.23	2.76	3.17
11	1.36	1.80	2.20	2.72	3.11
12	1.36	1.78	2.18	2.68	3.06
13	1.35	1.77	2.16	2.65	3.01
14	1.34	1.76	2.14	2.62	2.98
15	1.34	1.75	2.13	2.60	2.95
20	1.32	1.72	2.09	2.53	2.84
25	1.32	1.71	.2.06	2.48	2.79
30	1.31	1.70	2.04	2.46	2.75
∞	1.28	1.64	1.96	2.33	2.58

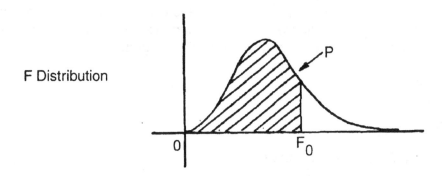

F Distribution

For given numbers of degrees of freedom and a given value of P, the table below gives the value F_0 for which $Pr\ (F < F_0) = P$.

Value of P	Degrees of freedom for denominator (lesser mean square)	Degrees of freedom for numerator (greater mean square)					
		5	6	7	8	9	10
0.950	5	5.05	4.95	4.88	4.82	4.77	4.74
0.975		7.15	6.98	6.85	6.76	6.68	6.62
0.990		11.0	10.7	10.5	10.3	10.2	10.1
0.995		14.9	14.5	14.2	14.0	13.8	13.6
0.950	6	4.39	4.28	4.21	4.15	4.10	4.06
0.975		5.99	5.82	5.70	5.60	5.52	5.46
0.990		8.75	8.47	8.26	8.10	7.98	7.87
0.995		11.5	11.1	10.8	10.6	10.4	10.2
0.950	7	3.97	3.87	3.79	3.73	3.68	3.64
0.975		5.29	5.12	4.99	4.90	4.82	4.76
0.990		7.46	7.19	6.99	6.84	6.72	6.62
0.995		9.52	9.16	8.89	8.68	8.51	8.38
0.950	8	3.69	3.58	3.50	3.44	3.39	3.35
0.975		4.82	4.65	4.53	4.43	4.36	4.30
0.990		6.63	6.37	6.18	6.03	5.91	5.81
0.995		8.30	7.95	7.69	7.50	7.34	7.21
0.950	9	3.48	3.37	3.29	3.23	3.18	3.14
0.975		4.48	4.32	4.20	4.10	4.03	3.96
0.990		6.06	5.80	5.61	5.47	5.35	5.26
0.995		7.47	7.13	6.88	6.69	6.54	6.42
0.950	10	3.33	3.22	3.14	3.07	3.02	2.98
0.975		4.24	4.07	3.95	3.85	3.78	3.72
0.990		5.64	5.39	5.20	5.06	4.94	4.85
0.995		6.87	6.54	6.30	6.12	5.97	5.85

1. On the average, 2 out of every 1,000 deaths in the United States are among people from 15 to 24 years of age. Use the Poisson distribution to approximate the probability that among a sample of 500 deaths, none is from this age group.

   A. 1/500
   B. e^{-2}
   C. $2e^{-2}$
   D. e^{-1}
   E. $2e^{-1}$

2. If $Pr(E_1) = p_1$, $Pr(E_2)\ p_2$ and if the sample space is $E_1 \cup E_2$, what is $Pr(E_1 \cap E_2)$?

   A. p_1p_2
   B. $p_1 + p_2$
   C. $1 - p_1 - p_2$
   D. $p_1 + p_2 - 1$
   E. $P_1 + p_2 - p_1p_2$

3. The probability density function of the random variable X is defined by

$$\begin{cases} f(x) = 3x^2, & 0 \leq x \leq 1, \\ f(x) = 0, & \text{elsewhere.} \end{cases}$$

   What is the probability that neither of two independent observations of X falls in the interval [1/3, 2/3]?

   A. 49/729
   B. 64/729
   C. 329/729
   D. 361/729
   E. 400/729

4. If $Pr(S) = p_8$, $Pr(T) = pt$ and the events S and T are independent, what is $Pr(S \cap T \backslash S)$?

   A. p_t
   B. p_8p_t
   C. $1 - p_8p_t$
   D. $1 - p_t + \dfrac{p_t}{p_8}$
   E. 1

5. A company annually uses many thousands of electric lamps which burn continuously day and night. Assume that under such conditions the life of a lamp may be regarded as a variable normally distributed about a mean of 50 days with a standard deviation of 19 days. On January 1, the company put 5,000 new lamps into service. How many (to the nearest 5) would be expected to need replacement by February 1?

   A. 270
   B. 395
   C. 795
   D. 855
   E. 1,705

6. The probability function of the discrete random variable X is defined by $f(x) = 2^{-x}$, $x = 1, 2, 3,$ ... ; $f(x) = 0$, elsewhere. What is the nth moment of X about the origin?

A. $\displaystyle\sum_{x=1}^{\infty} 2^{-x}$

B. $\displaystyle\sum_{x=1}^{\infty} 2^{-nx}$

C. $\displaystyle 2^{-n}\sum_{x-1}^{\infty} x^{n}$

D. $\displaystyle\sum_{x=1}^{\infty} x^{n} 2^{-x}$

E. $\displaystyle\sum_{x=1}^{\infty} n^{x} 2^{-x}$

Questions 7-8 refer to the random variable X whose probability density function is defined by

$$\begin{cases} f(x)=\dfrac{3}{x^4}, \ x\geq1; \\ f(x)=0, \ \text{elsewhere.} \end{cases}$$

7. What is the median of *X*?

    A. $\dfrac{1}{\sqrt[3]{2}}$

    B. $\sqrt{\dfrac{3}{2}}$

    C. $\sqrt[3]{2}$

    D. $\dfrac{3}{2}$

    E. 3

8. What is the mean of X?

    A. $\dfrac{3}{4}$

    B. $\sqrt{\dfrac{3}{2}}$

    C. $\sqrt[3]{2}$

    D. $\dfrac{3}{2}$

    E. 3

9. Given a bivariate distribution with $\mu_x = \mu_y = 0$, $\sigma_x = 2$, $\sigma_y = 1$ and a coefficient of correlation between x and y of 0.5, what is the coefficient of correlation between *x - y* and *y*?

    A. -0.5   B. -0.25
    C. 0   D. 0.25
    E. 1.0

10. One hundred cards numbered from 1 to 100 are shuffled and 2 cards are drawn without replacement. What is the probability that the greater of the 2 numbers drawn exceeds 50?

A. $\dfrac{137}{198}$

B. $\dfrac{3}{4}$

C. $\dfrac{149}{198}$

D. $\dfrac{7.599}{10.000}$

E. $\dfrac{629}{825}$

11. The x^2 test (without a correction for continuity) is to be applied to the contingency table

	$\overline{R}$	$\overline{\overline{R}}$	Total
$\overline{S}$	n	$100-n$	100
$\overline{\overline{S}}$	$100-n$	n	100
Total	100	100	200

to test the hypothesis that the two variables of classification are independent. If the test is conducted at the 5 per cent level of significance, the hypothesis will be accepted if and only if

A. $48 < n < 52$

B. $47 < n < 53$

C. $43 < n < 57$

D. $41 < n < 59$

E. $40 < n < 60$

12. Let X be the number of dots obtained when an unbiased die is thrown. For what number a is $E [X(a - X)]$ zero?

A. 0

B. 1

C. 3

D. 7/2

E. 13/3

13. The specific gravities of samples of a solution produced by a certain process are approximately normally distributed with mean 1.200 and standard deviation 0.010. Let the specific gravity of a sample selected at random be denoted by X. What is the order of relative magnitude of the probabilities defined below?

$$p_1 = pr(X \leq 1.196)$$

$$p_2 = pr(1.196 \leq X \leq 1.205)$$

$$p_3 = pr(1.205 \leq X)$$

A. $p_1 > p_3 > p_2$

B. $p_2 > p_1 > p_3$

C. $p_2 > p_3 > p_1$

D. $p_3 > P_1 > p_2$

E. $p_3 > p_2 > p_1$

14. For a set of n observed points (x_i, y_i) the following sums are known:

$$\frac{1}{n}\sum x_i = 2, \frac{1}{n}\sum y_i = 8; \frac{1}{n}\sum x_iy_i = 36; \quad \frac{1}{n}\sum x_i^2 = 29; \text{and } \frac{1}{n}\sum y_i^2 = 100$$ A line of the form $y = x + k$ is to be fitted to the n points by means of the method of least squares. What value of k should be used?

A. 4/5
B. 4
C. 6
D. 10
E. 6n

15. If an ordinary deck of 52 cards is dealt to four bridge players, what is the probability that the player who gets the ace of spades will also get the ace of hearts?

A. $\dfrac{1}{26}$

B. $\dfrac{1}{17}$

C. $\dfrac{4}{17}$

D. $\dfrac{1}{4}$

E. $\dfrac{13}{51}$

16. Each of three urns contains nine slips of paper numbered consecutively from 1 through 9. If one slip of paper is drawn at random from each urn, what is the probability that the sum of the numbers on the three slips will be odd?

A. $\dfrac{125}{729}$

B. $\dfrac{205}{729}$

C. $\dfrac{1}{2}$

D. $\dfrac{365}{729}$

E. $\dfrac{125}{243}$

17. What is the probability of finding the ace of hearts adjacent to the ace of diamonds in a well-shuffled deck of cards?

A. $\dfrac{1}{2.652}$

B. $\dfrac{1}{52}$

C. $\dfrac{1}{51}$

D. $\dfrac{1}{26}$

E. $\dfrac{2}{51}$

18. The only possible values of the random variable X are 1, 2, 3, . . . , 13. The probability of each is 1/13. The frequencies of occurrence of these values in a random sample of $13n$ observations are denoted by f_i (i = 1, 2, 3, ..., 13). If the value of the statistic $\frac{1}{n}\sum_{i-1}^{13}(f_i - n)^2$ is computed for each of 1,000 such samples, what is the expected number of samples for which this statistic will exceed 3.57?

    A. 10   B. 50
    C. 975   D. 990
    E. 995 .

19. Approximately how many times must a true coin be tossed before the probability of getting 53 per cent or more heads will be 1 per cent or less?

    A. 40   B. 380
    C. 730   D. 1,090
    E. 1,510

20. Each of the independent random variables $X1$, $X2$, . . . , Xn is distributed with mean μ and variance σ^2. If n is n large, for what value of c is $Pr(n\mu - c \le \sum_{i=1}^{n} X_i \le n\mu + c)$ approximately 0.99?

    A. $2.326\sigma\sqrt{n}$ B. $2.576\sigma\sqrt{n}$

    C. 2.576σ D. $2.326\dfrac{\sigma}{\sqrt{n}}$

    E. $2.576\dfrac{\sigma}{\sqrt{n}}$

21. What is the probability that it will be necessary to throw an unbiased die exactly n times in order to obtain exactly 2 fours?

    A. $\dfrac{(n-1)(n-2)}{2}\left(\dfrac{1}{6}\right)^2\left(\dfrac{5}{6}\right)^{n-2}$ B. $(n-1)\left(\dfrac{1}{6}\right)^2\left(\dfrac{5}{6}\right)^{n-2}$

    C. $n\left(\dfrac{1}{6}\right)^2\left(\dfrac{5}{6}\right)^{n-2}$ D. $\dfrac{n(n-1)}{2}\left(\dfrac{1}{6}\right)^2\left(\dfrac{5}{6}\right)^{n-2}$

    E. $\dfrac{n(n-1)}{2}\left(\dfrac{1}{6}\right)^2\left(\dfrac{5}{6}\right)^{n-2}$

22. The random variables $X_1, X_2, \ldots, X_n$ are identically and independently distributed with mean μ and variance σ^2. What is the variance of the random variable

$$\frac{\sum_{i-1}^{n} a_i X_i}{\sum_{i-1}^{n} a_i}, \text{ where } a_1, a_2, \ldots, a_n \text{ are constants?}$$

A. σ^2

B. $\left(\sum_i a_i^2\right)\sigma^2$

C. $\left(\sum_i a_i\right)^2 \sigma^2$

D. $\dfrac{\sum_i a_i^2}{\left(\sum_i a_i\right)^2}\sigma^2$

E. $\dfrac{\left(\sum_i a_i\right)^2}{\sum_i a_i^2}\sigma^2$

23. The moment generating function of the random variable X is defined by $M(t) = (1 - 2t)^{-n}$ (n a positive integer). What is the kth moment of X about the origin?

A. $2^k n(n+1) \ldots (n+k-1)$

B. $(-1)^k n(n+1) \ldots (n+k-1)$

C. $2^k \dfrac{(n+k-1)!}{(k-1)!}$

D. $2^k \dfrac{n!}{k!}$

E. $(1-2k)^{-n}$

24. The probability is p that there will be at least one accident in a certain factory in any given week. If the number of weekly accidents in this factory is Poisson-distributed, what is the mean number of weekly accidents?

A. $\dfrac{1}{P}$

B. $\dfrac{1}{1-P}$

C. $e^1 - P$

D. $-\ln$

E. $-\ln(1-p)$

25. A bag contains 2 unbiased coins and 1 two-headed coin. One of these 3 coins is chosen at random and tossed 4 times. Without examining both sides of the coin, it is noted that all 4 tosses are heads. What is the probability that the next toss will be a head?

A. $\dfrac{17}{32}$

B. $\dfrac{2}{3}$

C. $\dfrac{8}{9}$

D. $\dfrac{15}{16}$

E. $\dfrac{17}{18}$

26. The probability density function of the random variable X is given by

$$\begin{cases} f(x)=1, \ 0 \le x \le 1; \\ f(x)=0, \ \text{elsewhere.} \end{cases}$$

Let $Y = \sin X$. How is the probability density function of Y defined for $0 \le y \le \sin 1$?

A. $\dfrac{1}{\sin 1}$

B. $\sin y$

C. $\sin^{-1} y$

D. $\dfrac{1}{\sqrt{1-y^2}}$

E. $\sqrt{1-y^2}$

27. The random variables X, Y, U, V, have independent X2 distributions with nx, ny, nu, nv degrees of freedom, respectively. Which of the following describes the distribution of the random variable

$$\frac{(X+Y)/(n_x+n_y)}{(U+V)/(n_u+n_v)}?$$

A. X^2 with $(n_X + n_Y + n_U + n_V - 4)$ degrees of freedom
B. X^2 with $(n_X + n_Y - n_U - n_V - 4)$ degrees of freedom
C. F with the pair of degrees of freedom $(n_X + n_Y, n_U + n_V)$
D. F with the pair of degrees of freedom $(n_X + n_Y - 1, n_U + n_V - 1)$
E. F with the pair of degrees of freedom $(n_X + n_Y - 2, n_U + n_V - 2)$

28. A man alternately tosses an unbiased coin and throws an unbiased die, beginning with the coin. What is the probability that he will get a 3 or a 4 before he gets a head?

A. $\dfrac{1}{6}$

B. $\dfrac{1}{4}$

C. $\dfrac{1}{3}$

D. $\dfrac{2}{5}$

E. $\dfrac{1}{2}$

29. The probability density function of the random variable X is defined by

$$\begin{cases} f(x)=(\ln \theta)\,\theta^x, \ 0 \le x, \ 1<\theta; \\ f(x)=0, \ \text{elsewhere.} \end{cases}$$

What is the maximum likelihood estimator of the parameter 0 based on n independent observations..... $X_1, X_2, , X_n$?

A. $e^{n/\Sigma x_i}$

B. $e^{-\Sigma x_i/n}$

C. $e^{-n/\Sigma x_i}$

D. $\dfrac{\sum x_i}{n}$

E. $\dfrac{n}{\sum x_i}$

30. The probability density function of the random variable X is defined by

$$\begin{cases} f(x;\theta)=(\theta+1)x^\theta, 0 \leq x, \leq 1, \\ f(x;\theta)=0, \text{ elsewhere.} \end{cases}$$

where θ is an unknown nonnegative integer. A single random observation of X is to be used to test the hypothesis $H_0: \theta = n$ against the alternative hypothesis $H_1: \theta\ n+1$. Which of the following defines the best critical region of size 0.05 for this test?

A. $x \leq 1-\sqrt[n+1]{0.95}$

B. $x \leq \sqrt[n+1]{0.05}$

C. $x \geq 1-\sqrt[n+1]{0.05}$

D. $x \geq 1-\sqrt[n+1]{0.95}$

E. $\sqrt[n+1]{0.05} \leq x \leq \sqrt[n+1]{0.95}$

31. The random variables X and Y are independently distributed. The random variable X is normally distributed with mean μ. The random variable Y^2 has the x^2 distribution with n degrees of freedom. If the random variable has Student's t distribution with n degrees of freedom, what is the variance of X?

A. $\dfrac{1}{\sqrt{n}}$

B. 1

C. $\sqrt{n-1}$

D. $\sqrt{n}$

E. n

32. A certain industrial process yields a large number of steel cylinders whose lengths are approximately normally distributed with mean 3.25 inches and variance 0.0008 square inch. If two cylinders are chosen at random and placed end to end, what is the probability (to the nearest 0.01) that their combined length is less than 6.55 inches?

A. 0.84   B. 0.89   C. 0.95   D. 0.98   E. 0.99

33. A curve of the form $y=\lambda(x+\dfrac{1}{x})$ is to be fitted to the n observed points $(x_1, y_1), (x_2, y_2), \ldots ,$ (x_n, y_n) by the method of least squares. What value of X should be used?

A. $\dfrac{\sum_i y_i}{\sum_i (x_i + \frac{1}{x_i})}$

B. $\dfrac{\sum_i y_i^2}{\sum_i (x_i + \frac{1}{x_i})}$

C. $\dfrac{\sum_i y_i(x_i + \frac{1}{x_i})}{\sum_i (x_i + \frac{1}{x_i})}$

D. $\dfrac{\sum_i y_i(x_i + \frac{1}{x_i})}{\sum_i (x_i^2 + \frac{1}{x_i^2})}$

E. $\dfrac{\sum_i y_i(x_i + \frac{1}{x_i})}{\sum_i (x_i + \frac{1}{x_i})^2}$

34. The random variable X is such that $\Pr(a \le X \le b) = \dfrac{1}{a} \cdot \dfrac{1}{b}$ for $b \ge a \ge 1$.. How is the probability density function of X denned for $x \ge 1$?

A. $\dfrac{1}{x}$

B. $\dfrac{1}{x^2}$

C. $1 - \dfrac{1}{x}$

D. $1 - \dfrac{1}{x^2}$

E. $\ln x$

35. If X is a binomially distributed random variable with parameters n 162 and $p = 1/3$ and if ϕ is the cumulative normal distribution function with mean 0 and variance 1, what is the normal approximation to $Pr(X = 54)$?

A. $\phi(0)$

B. $\phi(\dfrac{1}{9\sqrt{2}}) - \phi(-\dfrac{1}{9\sqrt{2}})$

C. $\phi(\dfrac{1}{12}) - \phi(-\dfrac{1}{12})$

D. $\phi(\dfrac{1}{6}) - \phi(-\dfrac{1}{6})$

E. $\phi(\dfrac{1}{2}) - \phi(-\dfrac{1}{2})$

36. A random sample $(x_1, x_2, x_3, x_4, x_5)$ from a normal population gives $\bar{x} = 2500$ and $\sum_{i=1}^{5} (x_i - \bar{x})^2 = 80.00$ $(-\infty, \beta)$ is a 95 per cent confidence interval for the mean of the population, what is the value of β ?

A. 29.26
B. 30.14
C. 30.56
D. 34.08
E. 41.24

Questions 37-38 refer to the random variables X and Y whose joint probability density function is defined by

$$\begin{cases} f(x,y) = \frac{1+xy-y}{4}, & -1 \leq y \leq 1; \\ f(x,y) = 0, & \text{elsewhere.} \end{cases}$$

37. What is $pr(X \geq \frac{1}{2} | Y \leq -\frac{1}{2}) - pr(Y \geq \frac{1}{2} | X \leq -\frac{1}{2})$?

    A. 0

    B. $\frac{1}{64}$

    C. $\frac{1}{28}$

    D. $\frac{7}{16}$

    E. 1

38. What is the equation of the curve of regression of X on Y?

    A. $x - 1 = 0$
    B. $3x + 1 = 0$
    C. $6x - y + 1 = 0$
    D. $3y + 1 = 0$
    E. $6y - x + 1 = 0$

39. If the random variables X_1 and X_2 are independent and have equal variances, what is the coefficient of correlation between the random variables X_1 and $aX_1 + X_2$, where a is a constant?

    A. 0

    B. $\frac{1}{a}$

    C. a

    D. $\frac{1}{\sqrt{a^2+1}}$

    E. $\frac{a}{\sqrt{a^2+1}}$

40. Random samples of size 10 and 6 are drawn from normal populations P and Q, respectively. Unbiased estimates of the population variances are computed from the samples and denoted by $\hat{\sigma}_P^2$ and $\hat{\sigma}_Q^2$ ($\hat{\sigma}_P^2 > \hat{\sigma}_Q^2$). If the variances of the populations are equal, what is the probability that $\hat{\sigma}_P^2 > 10.2\hat{\sigma}_Q^2$?

    A. .005   B. .010   C. .050   D. .950   E. .995

41. The probability density function of the random variable X is defined by

$$\begin{cases} f(x) = 2x, & 0 \le x \le 1; \\ f(x) = 0, & \text{elsewhere.} \end{cases}$$

What is the moment generating function of X for $t \ne 0$?

A. $2te^t$

B. $\dfrac{e^t - 1}{t}$

C. $\dfrac{2}{t^2}(te^t - te^t)$

D. $\dfrac{te^t + e^t}{t^2}$

E. $\dfrac{2}{t^2}(1 - e^t + te^t)$

42. If $E(X) = 0$, $E(X^2) = \sigma^2$, $E(X^3) = 0$ and $E(X-1)^4 = 3\sigma^4 + 6\sigma^2 + 1$, what is $E(x^4)$?

A. $3\sigma^4$

B. $3\sigma^4 - 6\sigma^2 - 1$

C. $3\sigma^4 - 6\sigma^2$

D. $6\sigma^2 + 1$

E. $3\sigma^4 + 6\sigma^2 + 1$

43. If X is a binomially distributed random variable with parameters n and $1/2$, what is $E(X^2)$?

A. $\dfrac{n}{4}$

B. $\dfrac{n}{2}$

C. $\dfrac{n(n-1)}{4}$

D. $\dfrac{n2}{4}$

E. $\dfrac{n(n+1)}{4}$

Questions 44-45 refer to the random variable X whose probability density function is defined by

$$\begin{cases} f(x; \theta) = 1 + 2\theta - 3\theta x^2, & 0 \le x \le 1; \\ f(x; \theta) = 0, & \text{elsewhere.} \end{cases}$$

44. What is the maximum likelihood estimate of θ based on two independent observations, $1/2$ and 1?

A. $-\dfrac{3}{2}$

B. $-\dfrac{3}{4}$

C. $\dfrac{3}{4}$

D. 1

E. $3/2$

45. What is the power function of θ with respect to the critical region defined by $x < x_0 (0 < x_0 < 1)$?

    A. $1 + x_0(2 - 3x_0)\,\theta$ B. $x_0 + (x_0^2 - x_0^2)\,\theta$

    C. $(1 - x_0)(1 - x_0^2\,\theta)$ D. $(x_0^2 - x_0^2)\,\theta$

    E. $x_0 + x_0^2\,\theta - x_0^3\,\theta^2$

46. A random sample $(x_1, x_2,..., x_{10})$ from a normal population gives

$$\sum_{i=1}^{10} x_i = 10\bar{x} \text{ and } \sum_{i=1}^{10} (x_i - \bar{x})^2 = 1,000.$$ Which of the following is a 99 per cent confidence interval

for the mean of the population?

    A. $(\bar{x}-9.40, \bar{x}+9.40)$ B. $(\bar{x} - 10.83, \bar{x} + 10.83)$

    C. $(x - 27.64, x + 27.64)$ D. $(x - 28.21, x + 28.21)$

    E. $(x - 32.50, x + 32.50)$

Questions 47-49 refer to the pair of random variables *(X, Y)* which is uniformly distributed over the parallelogram with vertices (0, 0), (1,0), (1, 1), (2, 1).

47. What is $\Pr (Y \le \frac{1}{2} \mid X \le 1)$?

    A. $\dfrac{1}{8}$ B. $\dfrac{1}{4}$

    C. $\dfrac{3}{8}$ D. $\dfrac{1}{2}$

    E. $\dfrac{3}{4}$

48. How is the marginal probability density function of *X* defined for $0 \le x \le 2$

    A. $\dfrac{1}{2}, 0 \le x \le 2$ B. $\dfrac{1}{2}x, 0 \le x \le 2$

    C. $1 - \dfrac{1}{2}, 0 \le x \le 2$ D. $x, 0 \le x \le 1; 2-x, 1 < x \le 2$

    E. $\dfrac{1}{2}x^2, 0 \le x \le 1; 2-\dfrac{1}{2}x^2-1, 1 < x \le 2$

49. Let *Z* be the random variable *X + Y*. What is for $(Z \le z)$

    A. $1/4z$ B. $1/2z$

    C. $1/8z^2$ D. $1/4z^2$

    E. $1/2z^2$

50. The random variables $X_1, X_2, \ldots, X_n$ are independently distributed, each with moment generating function defined by $M(t) = e^{at^2}$ $(a \geq 0)$. How is the moment generating function of $\frac{1}{n}\sum_{i=1}^{n} X_i$ defined?

A. e^{at^2}

B. $\frac{1}{n}e^{at^2}$

C. $e^{(1/\sqrt{n})at^2}$

D. $e^{(1/n)at^2}$

E. e^{nat^2}

51. In controlling the quality of a manufactured product, care is taken to keep the mean of a certain variable at $\mu = 0$ and the standard deviation at $\sigma = \frac{1}{10}$. A random sample of 12 measurements $(x_1, x_2, \ldots, x_{12})$ is taken. Assume that the population mean, μ, has not changed and denote the sample mean by $\bar{x}$. What value must $\sum_{i-1}^{12}(x_i-\bar{x})^2$ exceed in order to reject at the 5 per cent significance level the hypothesis $\sigma = \frac{1}{10}$ in favor of the alternative hypothesis $\sigma > \frac{1}{10}$?

A. 0.046

B. 0.052

C. 0.197

D. 0.210

E. 0.219

52. If from a batch of 1,000 available questionnaires 80 random samples of 10 questionnaires each are drawn, each sample being replaced in the batch immediately after it has been drawn, what is the probability that no questionnaire will be drawn more than once in the entire sampling procedure?

A. $\dfrac{(990!)^{80}}{200!(1,000!)^{79}}$

B. $\dfrac{(990!)^{80}(10!)^{80}}{(1,000!)^{80}}$

C. $\dfrac{(10!)^{80}(990!)^{80}}{200!800!(1,000!)^{79}}$

D. $\dfrac{(990!)^{80}}{200!800!(1,000!)^{78}}$

E. $1-\dfrac{800}{(10)^{80}}$

53. The probability density function of the random variable X is defined by
$$\begin{cases} f(x) = e^{-x}, x \geq 0, \\ f(x) = 0, elsewhere. \end{cases}$$

44

Let Y be the second greatest observation in random samples of size 4 drawn from the distribution of X. Which of the following defines the probability density function of Y?

A. $4(1 - e^{-y})^3 e - y$

B. $12(1 - e^{-y})^2 e^{-2y} - 4(1 - e^{-y})^3 e^{-y}$

C. $12(1 - e^{-y})^2 e^{-2y}$

D. $4(1 - e^{-y})^3 e^{-y} + (1 - e^{-y})^4$

E. $12(1 - e^{-y}) e^{-3y}$

54. The final examination scores of 100 students have mean 50 and standard deviation 15. The term scores of these students have mean 60 and standard deviation 10. The coefficient of correlation between the two sets of scores is 0.8. Use a least-squares regression line to predict the final examination score for a student whose term score is 70.

A. 44.7

B. 55.3

C. 58

D. 62

E. 65

55. The random variables $X_1, X_2, \ldots, X_n$ are uniformly and independently distributed on [0, 1]. Let Y be the random variable max $\{X_1, X_2, \ldots, X_n\}$. What is the variance of Y?

A. $\dfrac{1}{12}$

B. $\dfrac{1}{12n}$

C. $\dfrac{1}{(n+1)(n+2)}$

D. $\dfrac{n}{(n+1)(n+2)}$

E. $\dfrac{n}{(n+1)^2(n+2)}$

KEY (CORRECT ANSWERS)

1. D	11. C	21. B	31. E	41. E	51. C
2. D	12. E	22. D	32. B	42. A	52. A
3. E	13. B	23. A	33. E	43. E	53. C
4. A	14. C	24. E	34. B	44. A	54. D
5. C	15. C	25. E	35. C	45. B	55. E
6. D	16. D.	26. D	36. A	46. B	
7. C	17. D	27. C	37. A	47. E	
8. D	18. D	28. B	38. B	48. D	
9. C	19. E	29. A	39. E	49. D	
10. C	20. B	30. D	40. B	50. D	

EXAMINATION SECTION
TEST 1

DIRECTIONS: Each question or incomplete statement is followed by several suggested answers or completions. Select the one that BEST answers the question or completes the statement. *PRINT THE LETTER OF THE CORRECT ANSWER IN THE SPACE AT THE RIGHT.*

1. If the median of a set of 45 marks is 82.5 and if the marks 100, 95, 40, and 15 are added to the set, the new median is   1.____

    A. 72.5   B. 77.0   C. 80.0   D. 82.5

2. The standard deviation of the set of scores 2, 5, 8 is equal to the standard deviation of which one of the following sets of scores?   2.____

    A. 4, 5, 6   B. 4, 25, 64   C. 4, 10, 16   D. 4, 7, 10

3. Assume that a jury panel contains 70 names, and among these are the names of Mr. C and Mr. D.
    If 12 jury men are to be selected by lot, the probability that BOTH Mr. C and Mr. D will be selected is   3.____

    A. 1/66   B. 22/805   C. 36/1225   D. 1/6

4. The odds in favor of getting a seven or an eleven on a single throw of a pair of dice are   4.____

    A. 1:9   B. 1:8   C. 2:9   D. 2:7

5. If the arithmetic mean of 40 marks is 72.5 and if four additional marks of 55, 65, 85, and 96 are added to the first 40, the new arithmetic mean is   5.____

    A. 72.00   B. 72.50   C. 72.70   D. 72.75

6. The statistic which is obtained from a set of N numbers x_i, (i = 1, 2...N) by the computation   6.____

    tion
    $$\frac{\sum\limits_{i=1}^{N} x_i}{N}$$

    is the set's

    A. median   B. arithmetic mean
    C. mode   D. standard deviation

7. A coin which may fall either heads or tails is tossed four times.
    The probability of getting at least one head is   7.____

    A. 3/4   B. 13/16   C. 7/8   D. 15/16

8. There are four test scores of which three are known to be 83, 82, and 72.
    If, using an assumed arithmetic mean of 80, the mean deviation of the four scores from the assumed mean is -2.25, the fourth score is   8.____

A. the smallest of the four
C. 76

B. 74
D. 79

9. The mean of a set of n numbers is equal to m, and the standard deviation is s. If each number of the set is tripled and then increased by 5, the mean and the standard deviation of the new set of numbers are, respectively,

9._____

A. m+5, 3s
C. 3m+5, 3s

B. 3m, 9s
D. 3m+5, 3s+5

10. How many even numbers greater than 40,000 may be formed using the digits 3, 4, 5, 6, and 9 if each digit must be used exactly once in each number?

10._____

A. 36　　　　B. 48　　　　C. 64　　　　D. 96

11. What is the probability of getting 80% or more of the questions correct on a five question true-false exam merely by guessing?

11._____

A. 1/16　　　　B. 5/32　　　　C. 3/16　　　　D. 7/32

12. Bag A contains 5 red and 4 black balls. Bag B contains 4 red and 6 black balls. If a bag is chosen at random and a ball is drawn from this bag, what is the probability that it will be black?

12._____

A. 4/15　　　　B. 10/19　　　　C. 47/90　　　　D. 7/10

13. The standard deviation of the measures -4, 8, 0, -3, 9 is CLOSEST to

13._____

A. 5.5　　　　B. 4.8　　　　C. 7.0　　　　D. 1.0

14. From a group of 5 men and 3 women, a committee of 2 is chosen. What is the probability that the committee will consist of 2 men?

14._____

A. 5/14　　　　B. 1/3　　　　C. 25/64　　　　D. 2/5

15. In how many ways can six people sit in a row if two particular ones are not to sit next to each other?

15._____

A. 240　　　　B. 360　　　　C. 480　　　　D. 720

16. The probability of drawing an ace or a heart from a standard deck of 52 cards, in a single drawing, is

16._____

A. 2/13　　　　B. 4/13　　　　C. 4/52　　　　D. 13/52

17. From among the following sets of scores,
　　　Set A 7, 2, 6, 7, 3
　　　Set B 7, 3, 9, 3, 8
　　　Set C 4, 3, 4, 5, 4
the one set in which the mode is greater than the median and the median is GREATER than the mean is

17._____

A. Set A
C. Set C

B. Set B
D. none of these

18. If a set of obtained measures is 8, 3, 5, 9, 13, 14, 22, 11, 2, 9, 8, 8, 18, which one of the following has the value 9?   18.____

    A.   Median   B.   Mode
    C.   Arithmetic mean   D.   Mean deviation

19. The standard deviation of the measures -6, 5, 0, -2, 8 is   19.____

    A.   1.00   B.   4.26   C.   4.98   D.   5.37

20. The probability that X will solve a problem is 1/3 and that Y will solve this problem is 4/5. If both work the problem independently, the probability the problem will be solved is   20.____

    A.   2/15   B.   4/15   C.   8/15   D.   13/15

KEY (CORRECT ANSWERS)

1.	D	11.	C
2.	D	12.	C
3.	B	13.	A
4.	D	14.	A
5.	D	15.	C
6.	B	16.	B
7.	D	17.	A
8.	B	18.	A
9.	C	19.	C
10.	A	20.	D

SOLUTIONS TO PROBLEMS

1. 82.5 must be the 23rd score, either counting from the highest to lowest or lowest to highest scores. By adding 100, 95, 40, and 15, 82.5 would still be the median since 24 scores lie below 82.5 and 24 scores lie above it. (Ans. D)

    1.____

2. Standard deviation = $\sqrt{\dfrac{\sum(x-\bar{x})^2}{N}}$. For 2, 5, 8 standard deviation = $\sqrt{6}$, which is exactly the same for the numbers 4, 7, 10. (Ans. D)

    2.____

3. The probability that C and D will be chosen first and second in either order is (2/70)(1/69). However, since a total of 12 will be selected, there are $_{12}C_2$ = 66 different combinations of selection numbers for C and D when both are chosen.
Final probability = 66(2/70)(1/69) = 22/805 . (Ans. B)

    3.____

4. There are a total of 8 combinations which will yield 7 or 11. There are a total of 36 combinations for both dice. Odds = probability of success ÷ probability of failure =

$$\frac{8}{36} \div \frac{28}{36} = 2{:}7. \quad \text{(Ans. D)}$$

    4.____

5. The total sum of all 40 marks = (72.5)(40) = 2900. By adding the four new numbers, the new total = 3201.
Then, 3201 ÷ 44 = 72.75. (Ans. D)

    5.____

6. The arithmetic mean is denoted by the sum of the numbers divided by the number of numbers. (Ans. B)

    6.____

7. Probability (at least one head) = 1 - Probability (no heads) = 1 - $(1/2)^4$ = 15/16 . (Ans. D)

    7.____

8. The mean deviation is the average of the absolute values (positive) of the differences between the raw scores and the mean. Assumed mean = 80. Mean deviation =-2.25 = 77.75 Four scores 83, 82, 72 and x must average 77.75. Fourth score is 74. (Ans. B)

    8.____

9. Each operation on the original numbers will affect the mean of those numbers in the same way. However, the standard deviation is NOT affected by adding a constant to each number. (Ans. C)

    9.____

10. If the first digit is 4, then the last digit must be 6 and there would be $_3P_3$ = 6 possibilities. Since 6 and 4 could be interchanged, there would be 6 possibilities of 6 _ _ _ 4.
But, if the first (highest) digit is 5 or 9, then the last digit could be 4 or 6, and the number of possibilities is $(2)(_3P_3)(2)$ = 24. Total number of possibilities = 6 + 6 + 24 = 36.
(Ans. A)

    10.____

11. Probability of 4 right = $_5C_4(.5)^4(.5)^1$ = .15625
Probability of 5 right = $_5C_5(.5)^5(.5)^0$ = .03125
The sum of these probabilities = .1875 = 3/16. (Ans. C)

    11.____

12. Let P = probability. P(black ball) = P(black ball from A) P(choosing A) + P(black ball from B). P(choosing B) = $\dfrac{4}{9} \cdot \dfrac{1}{2} + \dfrac{6}{10} \cdot \dfrac{1}{2} = \dfrac{47}{90}$. (Ans. C)

12.____

13. Standard deviation = $\sqrt{[n\sum x^2 - (\sum x)^2]/n^2} = \sqrt{[5(170)-100]/25} = \sqrt{30} = 5.5$ (Ans. A)

13.____

14. The total number of committees is $_8C_2 = \dfrac{8 \cdot 7}{2 \cdot 1} = 28$.

    The number of committees which will contain only men is $_5C_2 = \dfrac{5 \cdot 4}{2 \cdot 1} = 10$. Thus, the required probability = 10/28 or 5/14.
    Note: $_nC_R$ means the number of combinations of R objects from a group of n objects.

    Of course, n≥R. (Ans. A)

14.____

15. We want to eliminate all permutations where the two individuals would be both occupying seats 1 and 2, or seats 2 and 3, or .... or seats 5 and 6. This represents $10(_4P_4) = 240$. The total number of permutations = $_6P_6 = 6.5.4.3.2.4 = 720$. Thus, the number of acceptable arrangements = 480. (Ans. C)

15.____

16. There are 16 cards in the deck which are either a heart, an ace, or both. The probability = 16/52 = 4/13. (Ans. B)

16.____

17. In Set A, the mode = 7, median = 6, and mean = 5. (Ans. A)

17.____

18. When these numbers are arranged in ascending order, they appear as: 2, 3, 5, 8, 8, 8, 9, 9, 11, 13, 14, 18, 22. The median is the seventh number, which is 9. (Ans. A)

18.____

19. Standard deviation = $\sqrt{\sum(x-\bar{x})^2/n}$. Since $\bar{x} = 1$, this becomes $\sqrt{124/5} = 4.98$. (Ans. C)

19.____

20. Probability of either event = 1/3 + 4/5 - (1/3)(4/5) = 13/15. (Ans. D)

20.____

TEST 2

DIRECTIONS: Each question or incomplete statement is followed by several suggested answers or completions. Select the one that BEST answers the question or completes the statement. *PRINT THE LETTER OF THE CORRECT ANSWER IN THE SPACE AT THE RIGHT.*

1.   The number of ways in which 5 women and 1 man can be seated at a rectangular table at which the man may occupy only a position marked with an x is   1.____

    A.   60
    B.   120
    C.   240
    D.   360

2.   Four men, M, N, R, and S, stand in a row.   2.____
    The probability that M and N are next to each other is

    A.   1/6   B.   1/4   C.   1/3   D.   1/2

3.   The probability of obtaining 3 heads and 1 tail in a throw of 4 coins is   3.____

    A.   3/4   B.   1/2   C.   3/8   D.   1/4

4.   Mr. P.Q. Simpson is a football fan and says that there is a 70% probability that he will attend next Sunday's local football game if it does NOT snow, but only a 30% probability if it DOES snow. The weather bureau forecast is that there is a 60% chance that it will snow on Sunday.   4.____
    The probability that Mr. Simpson will attend the game on Sunday is

    A.   28%   B.   40%   C.   46%   D.   54%

5.   A teacher gave his class the problem of writing five, numbers whose mean, median, and mode are the same. Pupils A, B, C, and D obtained answers of, respectively,   5.____
    20,10,20,10,20; 10,2,16,12,10; 5,.05,5,50,5; and $1/2, 5 \times 10^{-1}, 3/4, .75, .5$.
    The CORRECT answer was that of Pupil

    A.   A   B.   B   C.   C   D.   D

6.   A box contains only red cards and black cards. If a card is selected at random from the box, the probability that it is red is 3/5.   6.____
    Which of the statements below is CORRECT?

    A.   The box contains 3 red cards and 2 black cards.
    B.   The box contains 3 red cards and 5 black cards.
    C.   If a card is selected at random from the box, the probability that it is black is 2/5.
    D.   If a card is selected at random from the box, the probability that it is black cannot be determined from the given information.

7.   If n and r represent positive integers and $n > r$, then $\dfrac{n(n-1)(n-2)...(n-r+1)}{1 \cdot 2 \cdot 3 \cdot ....r}$ is an integer   7.____

    A.   *only* if n is composite
    B.   *only* if r divides n
    C.   *only* if n is composite and r divides n
    D.   for all values of n and r

8. In a survey of the population of the village of Great Neck, it was found that 27% of the population needed eyeglasses, 14% of the population were left-handed, and 5% needed eyeglasses and were also left-handed.
   What percent of the population of Great Neck neither needed eyeglasses nor were left-handed?

   A. 54   B. 59   C. 64   D. 69

   8.____

9. The odds AGAINST throwing an 8 in a single roll with two dice is

   A. 36 to 5   B. 5 to 1   C. 6 to 1   D. 31 to 5

   9.____

10. A set of students' marks on a quiz worth ten points was as follows: 2, 2, 3, 3, 5, 5, 5, 7, 7, 7, 7, 9, 10. The arithmetic mean, median, and mode of this set of marks, arranged in descending order of magnitude, will be

    A. median, mode, arithmetic mean
    B. mode, arithmetic mean, median
    C. mode, median, arithmetic mean
    D. arithmetic mean, median, mode

    10.____

11. Three *fair* coins are tossed.
    What is the probability of getting exactly two heads?

    A. 3/8   B. 1/8   C. 2/3   D. 1/2

    11.____

12. Two *fair* coins are tossed.
    The probability that both coins show heads is

    A. 1   B. 3/4   C. 1/2   D. 1/4

    12.____

13. The number of permutations of the elements of the set $\{x_1, x_2, ..., x_n\}$, using all the elements of the set in each permutation, is

    A. 2^n B. n^2 C. $n!$ D. $\sum_{i=1}^{n} x_i$

    13.____

14. A box contains only red cards and black cards. If a card is selected at random from the box, the probability that it is red is 4/7.
    Which of the statements below is CORRECT?

    A. The box contains 4 red cards and 7 black cards.
    B. If a card is selected at random from the box, the probability that it is black cannot be determined from the given information.
    C. The box contains 4 red cards and 3 black cards.
    D. If a card is selected at random from the box, the probability that it is black is 3/7.

    14.____

15. A box contains 3 white balls and 2 red balls. If a ball is drawn at random and not replaced and a second ball is drawn at random, what is the probability that both balls are red?

    A. 1/10   B. 2/25   C. 2/5   D. 13/20

    15.____

KEY (CORRECT ANSWERS)

1.	C	6.	C
2.	B	7.	D
3.	D	8.	C
4.	C	9.	D
5.	B	10.	B

11.	A
12.	D
13.	C
14.	D
15.	A

———

SOLUTIONS TO PROBLEMS

1. The number of ways of seating the man = $_2P_1$ = 2.
   The number of ways of seating the 5 women = $_5P_5$ = 120.
   The total number of arrangements of all people = (2)(120) = 240. (Ans. C)

2. There are $_4P_4$ = 24 ways in which M, N, R, and S can be arranged in a row. There are 6 ways in which M and N are next to each other. The required probability is 6/24 = 1/4. (Ans. B)

3. Probability of any 3 heads and 1 tail out of 4 coins = $_4C_3$ $(1/2)^3(1/2)$ = (4)(1/16) = 1/4. (Ans. D)

4. Probability = (.70)(.40) + (.30)(.60) = .46 = 46%. (Ans. C)

5. Pupil B's example has a mean, median, and mode = 10. (Ans. B)

6. Probability of a black card = 1 - 3/5 = 2/5 . (Ans. C)

7. Recognize that $\dfrac{n(n-1)(...)(n-r+1)}{(1)(2)(...)(r)} = _nC_R$ which is the number of combinations of n items taken r at a time. $_nC_R$ must always be an integer. (Ans. D)

8. Let A = event that a person needs glasses, B = event that a person is left-handed. Then, P(A) = .27, P(B) = .14, and $P(A \cap B)$ = .05. Then, $P(A \cup B)$ = .27 + .14 - .05 = .36.
   This means that 36% of the people either need glasses or are left-handed or both.
   Thus, 64% fall into neither category. (Ans. C)

9. Probability of rolling an 8 = 5/36 , so probability of NOT rolling an 8 = 31/36 . This translates to odds of 31 to 5. (Ans. D)

10. Mean = 72/13 = 5.54. Mode = 7 Median = 5
    The descending order is mode, mean, median. (Ans. B)

11. Probability (exactly 2 heads) = (3)(probability of getting heads on 2 specific coins) = (3)(1/8) = 3/8. (Ans. A)

12. Probability = $(1/2)^2$ = 1/4. (Ans. D)

13. The number of permutations of n elements (using all elements) = n(n-1)(n-2)(...)(1) = n! (Ans. C)

14. Probability of selecting a red card + probability of selecting a black card = 1. Thus, the required probability = 1 - 4/7 = 3/7. (Ans. D)

15. Probability (2 red balls) = (2/5) (1/4) = 1/10.(Ans. A)

1.____
2.____
3.____
4.____
5.____
6.____
7.____
8.____
9.____
10.____
11.____
12.____
13.____
14.____
15.____

EXAMINATION SECTION
TEST 1

DIRECTIONS: Each question or incomplete statement is followed by several suggested answers or completions. Select the one that BEST answers the question or completes the statement. *PRINT THE LETTER OF THE CORRECT ANSWER IN THE SPACE AT THE RIGHT.*

1. In the binary system (using digits 0 and 1), the decimal system number 232 is written as   1.____

    A.   1010101   B.   1110100   C.   11101000   D.   11101010

2. The following data is for a firm selling cigarettes, cigars, and pipe tobacco for the year   2.____
2019, and the average for the base years 2017-19.

	Quantity in		Price in	
	2017-19	2019	2017-19	2019
Cigarettes	7,000	8,000	2.20	2.50
Cigars	1,100	1,000	3.10	3.40
Pipe tobacco	900	1,000	0.90	0.80

The 2019 index number (2017-19 = 100) for total sales is

    A.   123   B.   120   C.   112   D.   110

3. Given the following data: 3.____

	Country A		Country B
Age Group	Population	Death Rate Per 1,000	Population
0-24	1,200,000	1.7	2,400,000
25-64	2,500,000	7.2	3,000,000
65 and over	300,000	125.0	600,000

If the death rates in each age group in Country B are the same as in Country A, then the ratio of the total crude death rate in Country A over that for Country B is MOST NEARLY

    A.   .80   B.   .86   C.   1.17   D.   1.20

4. If $B(m,n) = \int_0^1 x^{m-1}(1-x)^{n-1}\,dx$ and $x = (1+y)^{-1}$, then $B(m,n)$ in terms of y equals   4.____

    A. $\int_0^\infty \dfrac{y^{n-1}dy}{(1+y)^{m+n}}$

    B. $\int_0^\infty -\dfrac{y^{m-1}dy}{(1+y)^{m+n}}$

    C. $\int_0^1 \dfrac{y^m\,dy}{(1+y)^{m+n-2}}$

    D. $\int_0^\infty \dfrac{y^{m-1}\,dy}{(1+y)m+n-2}$

5. If there are n values of X_i and Y_i, and ξX_i and ξY_i stands for the sum of all values from i   5.____
= 1 to i = n, and $\bar{X} = \xi \dfrac{X_i}{n}$ and $\bar{Y} = \dfrac{Y_i}{n}$, then the ξ $(X_i-X)(Y_i-Y)$ equals

A. $\xi X_i Y_i - n\overline{XY}$ B. $n\xi X_i Y_i - \xi X_i \xi Y_i$

C. $\xi X_i Y_i - \xi X_i \xi Y_i$ D. $\xi X_i Y_i - 3\overline{XY}$

6. Given the Cogg-Douglas function: $x = al^b k^c$. Assume $X = \log x$, $A = \log a$, $B = \log b$, $K = \log k$, $L = \log 1$, $C = \log c$, then $X =$ 6.____

     A. $a + bL + CK$ B. $A + BL + CK$

     C. $A \cdot B \cdot C \cdot L \cdot K$ D. $A + bL + cK$

7. When the forecast of the meteorologist at the Weather Bureau is based on the compila-   7.____
tion of all available meteorological data is indicative of the strength of his belief as an
expert, this MOST directly exemplifies the _____ approach to probability.

     A. classical   B. conditional

     C. relative frequency   D. subjective

8. A sample of 8 students from a class of 40 are selected at random and 5 are boys and 3   8.____
are girls. The probability of this result, if it is known that there are 20 girls in the class, is

     A. .375   B. .237   C. .23   D. .21

9. A department head calls in three of his bureau chiefs to help him determine whether or   9.____
not to make a certain decision. From past experience, he knows that two of his bureau
chiefs are wrong 5 percent of the time and that the third is wrong 10 percent of the time.
He decides to make the decision proposed by the majority. His decision will then be
wrong _____ percent of the time.

     A. 0.25   B. 0.5   C. 1.2   D. 6.7

10. The performances of an experienced stock market analyst is being studied. From past   10.____
records we determine that when he predicts the market will rise, it rises 70 percent of the
time and when he predicts it will fall, it falls 80 percent of the time. If during the period in
question the market is rising 90 percent of the time, the posterior probability that the market will actually fall on a day that he predicts a drop is

     A. .20   B. .23   C. .30   D. .31

11. In consumer sampling, if we have reason to believe that there are important differences   11.____
in consumer attitudes according to age and sex, then the sampling procedure that would
probably be MOST desirable is the _____ sample.

     A. cluster   B. simple random

     C. stratified   D. systematic

12. In the conduct of a survey, statistical theory provides the bases by which the senior stat-   12.____
istician can BEST

     A. determine how the nonsampling errors affect the results

     B. determine the sampling errors that result from a probability sample of the prese-
        lected frame

     C. evaluate the content of the questionnaire

     D. go from the frame to the universe

13. In a complicated systematic, stratified, cluster sampling design, the BEST and SIM-   13.____
    PLEST formulas for the standard error can be obtained from the theory of

    A.   cohort analysis   B.   multi-stage sampling
    C.   replicated sampling   D.   sequential sampling

14. If a die is thrown 105 times, then the sum of the expected mean plus the standard devia-   14.____
    tion of the mean equals MOST NEARLY

    A.   6 1/12   B.   6 5/12   C.   3 1/2   D.   3 2/3

15. The size of the sample that is required to determine whether a Democrat or Republican   15.____
    will win a certain election within .3 percent accuracy with 95.4 percent confidence is

    A.   1,000   B.   1,111   C.   10,329   D.   11,111

16. In a cluster sample, it is desirable that each cluster be   16.____

    A.   heterogeneous and the differences between clusters be homogeneous
    B.   homogeneous and the different clusters be heterogeneous
    C.   homoscedastic and the different clusters be hetero-scedastastic
    D.   just like every other cluster

Questions 17-18.

DIRECTIONS: Questions 17 and 18 are to be answered on the basis of the following information.

Given the following population:
    Stratum I: 3, 4, 4, 6, 6, 7
    Stratum II: 8, 8, 12, 15, 17, 18
    Stratum III: 16, 16, 18, 22, 22, 26

and the interview cost in Stratum I is $1 per interview, $4 for Stratum II, and $9 for Stratum
III.

17. A sample of size n = 10 selected by optimum allocation would have the following sam-   17.____
    ple from each stratum:

    A.   3, 5, 2   B.   3, 4, 3   C.   2, 5, 3   D.   2, 4, 4

18. If the variance of $\overline{X}$ in the above question is given by the formula,   18.____

$$V(\overline{X})=\sum_{k=1}^{k=3} \frac{N_k - n_k}{N_k - 1} = \frac{(N_k S_k)^2}{n_k}$$

where N_k is the universe number in stratum nk, k = the number sampled and S_k is the

standard deviation in stratum k, then V($\overline{X}$) equals MOST NEARLY

    A.   1.08   B.   10.8   C.   10.9   D.   180

19. In an investigation of the effect of diet on the incidence of heart disease, a senior statisti-   19.____
    cian made a detailed survey of 1,000 men selected at random over a 10-year period. The
    group received regular, thorough, physical examinations. The senior statistician con-
    cluded that the diet lowered the cholesterol level of all members of the group. His investi-
    gation is MOST seriously defective since he

A. had no control group for comparison
B. did not show in his results that the incidence of heart disease was lowered
C. did not show that his group did not develop other serious illnesses
D. did not compute the sampling errors

20. A 30 percent response was secured after 5 mailings in a nationwide follow-up sample survey of 30,000 persons who graduated from high school 5 years before. Under these circumstances, the statistician in charge of this survey should BEST recommend that   20.____

A. substitution of other graduates in the same areas be made and mail questionnaires sent to the substitutes
B. the survey should be scrapped
C. the 9,000 returns are adequate and should be used as the final report
D. an intensive follow-up by telephone and personal visit be made of 5 percent of the nonrespondents

21. One way to determine the extent of interviewer bias is to compute $\sim$ - the average intra-class correlation between interviews within investigators. If g is_the number of interviews   21.____

per investigator, then Var $(\overline{X})= \dfrac{G2}{g}[(1+\sim(g-1)]$, where without such bias Var

$(\overline{X}) = \dfrac{G2}{g}$.

Assuming that each investigator does 101 interviews and $\sim$ = .03, then a self-filled questionnaire sample without interviewer bias would give the same results as an interviewer sample of _____ percent.

A. 50   B. 33 1/3   C. 25   D. 10

22. In many sample research studies, the investigator compares the results for a control group and an experimental group solely in terms of the differences between the averages of the 2 groups. This procedure is defective PRIMARILY because   22.____

A. both measures may contain biases
B. differences may frequently result from the presence of sampling errors
C. small differences are statistically significant
D. the sampling designs are faulty

23. A common method to check on the validity of a sample is to check some characteristic against known total figures obtained from a complete count, such as a census or an accounting tabulation. This is NOT a valid test because   23.____

A. the greater detailed tabulations obtained from the sample makes it easier to spot inaccuracies
B. the size of the universe determines the size of the sample
C. the nonsampling errors in a complete count are frequently greater than the sampling plus nonsampling errors of the sample
D. modern computing machines eliminate most of the non-sampling errors in samples

24. A research survey is to be made by a team of psychologists and you are the consulting   24.____
senior statistician. Your functions will MOST likely include the

  A. decision as to whether or not the proposed frame is satisfactory
  B. determination of the type of statistical information to be obtained
  C. rules for coding the data and the actual coding
  D. selection of the sample and the computation of estimates and standard errors

25. A survey was made in 22 cities before and after a heavy advertising campaign for a cer-   25.____
tain product. The results showed that about 71.9 percent were aware of the product
before advertising and 74.2 percent afterwards. About 1,000 persons were interviewed
by telephone before and a different 1,000 persons after the campaign. The non-response
rate was about 60 percent in each case. From this statement of the project, it can be said
that

  A. the difference of 2.3 percent is significant
  B. a smaller sample would have produced better results
  C. no valid probability statement can be made of the effectiveness of the advertising
  D. nothing could be done about the non-response

KEY (CORRECT ANSWERS)

1.	C	11.	C
2.	A	12.	B
3.	B	13.	C
4.	A	14.	D
5.	A	15.	B
6.	D	16.	A
7.	D	17.	A
8.	C	18.	C
9.	C	19.	A
10.	B	20.	D

21.	C
22.	B
23.	C
24.	D
25.	C

SOLUTIONS TO PROBLEMS

1. CORRECT ANSWER: C
In the binary system, counting from right to left, the placeholders are 1, 2, 4, 8, 16, 32, 64, 128,.... Since 232 = (1)(128) + (1)(64) + (1)(32) + (0)(16) + (1)(8) + (0)(4) + (0)(2) + (0)(1), the binary form of 232 is 11101000.

2. CORRECT ANSWER: A
The total sales for 2017-19 = (7000)(2.20) + (1100)(3.10) + (900)(.90) = $19,620. The total sales for 2019 = (8000)(2.50) + (1000)(3.40) + (1000)(.80) = $24,200. The index number for 2019 = (24,200/19,620)(100) = 123 (rounded off).

3. CORRECT ANSWER: B
<u>Country A</u>
Population: 1,200,000 + 2,500,000 + 300,000 = 4,000,000
Deaths:

$$1,200,000 \times \frac{1.7}{1000} = 2,040$$

$$2,500,000 \times \frac{7.2}{1000} = 18,000$$

$$300,000 \times \frac{125}{1000} = 37,500$$
Total = 57,540

Total/million: $\frac{57,540}{4} = 14,385$

<u>Country B</u>
Population: 2,400,000 + 3,000,000 + 600,000 = 6,000,000
Deaths:

$$2,400,000 \times \frac{1.7}{1000} = 4,080$$

$$3,000,000 \times \frac{7.2}{1000} = 21,600$$

$$600,000 \times \frac{125}{1000} = 75,000$$
Total = 100,680

Total/million: $\frac{100,680}{6} = 16,780$

$$\frac{\text{Death rate country A}}{\text{Death rate country B}} = \frac{14,385}{16780} = .857 = .86$$

4. CORRECT ANSWER: A

$$B(m,n) = \int_0^1 x^{m-1}(1-x)^{n-1}\, dx \qquad x = (1+y)^{-1}, \text{ then}$$

B(m,n) in terms of y equals $\qquad$ x=0 $\qquad$ x = 1

$$x = \frac{1}{1+y} \qquad\qquad\qquad (1+y)^{-1} = 0 \quad (1+y)^{-1} = 1$$

$$dx = \frac{1}{(1+y)^2}\, dy \qquad\qquad \frac{1}{1+y} = 0 \quad \frac{1}{1+y} = 1$$

$$x^{m-1} = (\frac{1}{1+y})^{m-1} = \frac{(1+y)}{(1+y)^m} \qquad y+1 = \frac{1}{0} = \infty \quad y = 0$$

$$(1-x)^{n-1} = [1 - (\frac{1}{1+y})]^{n-1} \qquad\qquad y = \infty$$

$$= [\frac{y}{1+y}]^{n-1}$$

$$B(m,n) = \int_\infty^0 \frac{(1+y)}{(1+y)^m} \cdot \frac{y^{n-1}}{(1+y)^{n-1}} \cdot \frac{(-1)1}{(1+y)^2}\, dy$$

$$= \int_\infty^0 \frac{y^{n-1}\, dy}{(1+y)^{m+n}}$$

5. CORRECT_ANSWER: A

$$\xi(X_i - \overline{X})(Y_i - \overline{Y}) = \xi(X_iY_i) - \xi\,\overline{X}Y_i - \xi\,YX_i + \xi\overline{XY}$$

$$= \xi X_iY_i - \overline{X}\xi Y_i - \overline{Y}\xi X_i + n\overline{XY}$$

$$= \xi X_iY_i - n\overline{XY} - n\overline{XY} + \hbar\,\overline{XY} = \xi X_iY_i - n\overline{XY}$$

6. CORRECT ANSWER: D

$$a\tilde{\ell}^b k^c, \text{ so } \log x = X = \text{Log}[a\ell^b k^c]$$

$$= \text{Log } a + b\text{Log } \ell + c\text{Log } k = A + bL + cK$$

7. CORRECT ANSWER: D

Whenever a person utilizes his personal belief on a question involving probability, this illustrates a subjective approach.

8. CORRECT ANSWER: C

$$\frac{20C_5 \cdot 20C_3}{40C_8} = 2298$$

$$\text{Numerator} = \frac{20\times19\times18\times17\times16\times20\times19\times18}{5\times4\times3\times2 \ \times \ 3\times2\times1}$$

$$= \frac{19\times3\times17\times16\times20\times19\times3}{19}$$

$$\text{Denominator} = \frac{40 \times 39 \times 38 \times 37 \times 36 \times 35 \times 34 \times 33}{2 \times 7 \times 6 \times 5 \times 4 \times 3 \times 2 \times 1} = .2298$$

9. CORRECT ANSWER: C

Assume that the first two chiefs are wrong .05 of the time and the third chief is wrong .10 of the time. P (wrong decision for dept. head) = P (1st chief wrong) P (2nd chief wrong) P (3rd chief right) + P (1st chief wrong) P (2nd chief right) - P (3rd chief wrong) + P (1st chief right) P (2nd chief wrong) P (3rd chief wrong) + P (all 3 chiefs wrong) = $(.05)^2(.90)$ + $(.05)(.95)(.10)$ + $(.95)(.05)(.10)$ + $(.05)^2(.10)$ = .012.

10. CORRECT ANSWER: B

We have P(A|B) = .70, P(A'|B) = .30, P(B) = .90, P(B') = .10, where A = predicts market will rise, B = market does rise, A' = predicts market will fall. B' = market does fall. We also know that P(A'|B') = .80. Then, P(B'|A') = P(B').P(A'|B')/ [P(B').P(A'|B') + P(B) P(A'|B)] =

(.10)(.80)/[(.10)(.80) + (.90)(.30)] = .08/.35 $\approx$ .23.

11. CORRECT ANSWER: C

In this type of sampling, the actual sample is selected from specific categories, such as age and sex. The sample would include both genders and individuals of different ages.

12. CORRECT ANSWER: B

In any statistically-related surveys, errors will occur. The statistician must be able to identify these errors, by way of statistical theory.

13. CORRECT ANSWER: C

Replication permits estimating the experimental error and also provides for minimizing it. This type of sampling yields best results for a standard error.

14. CORRECT ANSWER: D

The mean = 1(1/6) + 2(1/6) + 3(1/6) + 4(1/6) + 5(1/6) + 6(1/6) = 3.5. The standard deviation of the mean =

$$\sqrt{(0^2 \cdot 1/6 + 1^2 \cdot 1/6 + 2^2 \cdot 1/6 + 3^2 \cdot 1/6 + 4^2 \cdot 1/6 + 5^2 \cdot 1/6 + 6^2 \cdot 1/6 - (3.5)^2]/105} = .1\overline{6}. = .16.$$

So, 3.5 + .1$\overline{6}$ = 3 2/3

15. CORRECT ANSWER: B

Z, -6 The formula is n = $(\frac{Z_{\alpha/2} \cdot \delta}{E})^2$, where n = required number,

$Z_{\alpha/2}$ = critical Z value of a normal distribution, δ = standard deviation, and E = error.

Thus, n = $(\frac{2 \cdot \frac{1}{2}}{.03})^2 = (33.\overline{3})^2 \approx 1111$. We assume that $\delta = \frac{1}{2}$.

16. CORRECT ANSWER: A

In cluster sampling, each cluster will represent a cross-section of a desired trait. However, all clusters will share these cross-sections.

17. CORRECT ANSWER: A
The_expected value of any sample of each strata are:

$E \overline{X}_I = 5$, $E \overline{X}_{II} = 13$, $E \overline{X}_{III} = 20$. The expected cost for

stratum I = ($1)(5)(13) + ($4)(13)(5) + ($9)(20)(2) = $635, wich choice A. This is lower than the values of choices B, C, or D, which are respectively $763, $810, and $938.

18. CORRECT ANSWER: C

19. CORRECT ANSWER: A
A control group is necessary in order to make sound comparisons.

20. CORRECT ANSWER: D
This procedure would raise the response rate to 35%, which should yield a fairly accurate set of results.

21. CORRECT ANSWER: C

With bias on the part of the interviewer, $V(\overline{X}) = \dfrac{\delta^2}{100} [1 + (.03)(100)]$

$= \dfrac{4\delta^2}{100} = \delta^2/25$. Without bias, $V(\overline{X}) = \delta^2/100$. The ratio of $\delta^2/100 \div \delta^2/25$ reduces to 1/4 or 25%.

22. CORRECT ANSWER: B
This is especially true if random sampling was used, because any outliers would definitely affect the value of the average.

23. CORRECT ANSWER: C
Whereas sampling errors are due to a poor sampling plan which does not contain a truly accurate picture of the population, non-sampling errors are the result of inaccurate observations. The latter type of errors of a population would normally exceed, in count, both types of errors for any particular sample.

24. CORRECT ANSWER: D
The statistician is more concerned with sample selection and subsequent analysis than with methods of coding data or with the type of data being sought.

25. CORRECT ANSWER: C
Since only about 400 people responded, the actual numbers represented by 71.9% and 74.2% are 288 and 297, respectively. This is hardly significant, with 600 non-respondents.

TEST 2

DIRECTIONS: Each question or incomplete statement is followed by several suggested answers or completions. Select the one that BEST answers the question or completes the statement. *PRINT THE LETTER OF THE CORRECT ANSWER IN THE SPACE AT THE RIGHT.*

1. If you had to determine the extent and impact of automation in a metropolitan city industry, the BEST way to proceed would be to

    A. do a two-stage sample survey. The first stage would be a comprehensive, sample mail survey to determine the presence of the equipment and the second stage would involve intensive interviewing of those who reported that they had such equipment
    B. do a comprehensive library research job of the literature for instances of the uses of automation in this city and then do a field follow-up of those firms that have it
    C. study all previous surveys and do an intensive job in those industries and size groups where automation may be prevalent
    D. design a detailed, comprehensive questionnaire and send it to all firms in this city

1.____

2. A certain drug is known to produce nausea in about 1 percent of the patients in the general population. A doctor gave this drug to 100 of his patients with a certain disease and since none of them complained of nausea, he concluded that the drug was perfectly safe to use. His conclusions were invalid in that such a result would obtain only for samples of 100 about _____ percent of the time.

    A. 10   B. 37   C. 63   D. 95

    NOTE: Use the Poisson distribution $\dfrac{m^x e^{-m}}{x!}$, where m = N.p and e = 2.718.

2.____

3. If $r_{12.3} = \dfrac{r_{12} - r_{13} r_{23}}{\sqrt{(1-r_{13}^2)(1-r_{23}^2)}}$ and r_{12} = .3, r_{13} .1, and r_{23} = .5 than $r_{12.3}$ equals

    A. .29   B. .31   C. .42   D. .65

3.____

4. If $r_{12} = r_{23} = r_{34} = {\sim}$ and $r_{13} = r_{24} = {\sim}^2$, and $r_{14} = {\sim}^3$, then the partial correlation coefficients $r_{13.2}$, $r_{14.2}$, $r_{24.3}$ and $r_{14.3}$ are all

    A. equal to 0
    B. except $r_{14.3}$ equal to 0
    C. except $r_{13.2}$ equal to 1
    D. equal to 1

4.____

5. If the seasonal index for a time series is 120 in a given month, this means that the

    A. average of the seasonal indices for the other 11 months is 80
    B. seasonal index for that month is higher than at least half of the other months
    C. seasonal index for at least one other month must be below 100
    D. unadjusted data for the month is increased 20 percent when seasonally adjusted

5.____

6. If an employment series is declining over a period of time, then the linear regression equation ($y = a+bt$) where it is positive for all years MUST have

   A. a negative a and positive b
   B. a positive a and negative b
   C. either a positive or negative a and a negative b
   D. either a positive or negative a and a positive or negative b

   6.____

7. The one of the following statements concerning the normal distribution which is false is that the

   A. normal distribution has exceptionally convenient properties which have made it the model for much of statistical theory
   B. normal distribution is the one unifying model for the representation of the random variation in all measurable natural phenomena
   C. many non-normal distributions approach normality under certain limiting conditions which can be frequently simulated in practical situations
   D. random variation of many natural phenomena can be represented by the normal distribution to a high degree of accuracy

   7.____

8. In testing the hypothesis that r means are equal, of the following, the analysis of variance technique does NOT assume that

   A. an equal number of observations be made from each of the r populations
   B. the r samples are drawn randomly
   C. the r populations are normal
   D. the r population variances are equal

   8.____

9. Given the matrix of simple correlations,

   $$R = \begin{vmatrix} r_{11} & r_{12} & r_{13} \\ r_{12} & r_{22} & r_{23} \\ r_{13} & r_{23} & r_{33} \end{vmatrix}$$

   and that the multiple coefficient of determination $R^2_{123} = 1 - R/R_{11}$, where R is the value of the above determinant and R_{11} is the cofactor of r_{11}, which equals $1 - r^2_{23}$, if $r_{11} = r_{22} = r_{33} = 1$ and $r_{12} = .5$, $r_{13} = -.5$, and $r_{23} = 0$, then $R^2_{1.23}$ equals

   A. 0   B. 1/3   C. 1/4   D. 1/2

   9.____

10. To test the hypothesis that the number of storks and the birth rate are independent, the following data have been gathered:

Countries With	Number of Storks		
	Few	Many	Total
Small birth rate	50	10	60
Large birth rate	150	40	190
Total	200	50	250

   The value of x^2 used to test this hypothesis is

   A. .54   B. .55   C. 1.37   D. 5.5

   10.____

11. The criterion for choosing a point estimator which can be represented by the mean X for the sample approaches u, the mean for the universe as the sample size n approaches the universe size N is that of   11.____

    A. unbiasedness   B. sufficiency
    C. efficiency   D. consistency

12. In a positively skewed distribution of measurements, the _____ is larger than the _____ .   12.____

    A. mean; median   B. median; mean
    C. mode; mean   D. mode; median

13. Discriminant analysis is that branch of statistics which attempts to   13.____

    A. accept or reject a given hypothesis based on sample data
    B. classify an individual as belonging to one or two populations p_1, or p_2 on the basis of a number of measurements made on him
    C. determine the amount of discrimination prevalent in an area
    D. determine the classification of an individual through his characteristics without error

14. A computed chi-square value with a negative sign   14.____

    A. has to be interpreted in terms of the defined significance level
    B. always indicates that the observed differences, if any, are significant
    C. always indicates that the observed differences, if any, are insignificant
    D. is mathematically impossible

15. In locating the position of the mode within a class of grouped data, it is assumed that the measurements located in the model class are   15.____

    A. all located at the midpoint of the class
    B. dispersed according to the frequencies in the two adjoining classes
    C. dispersed equally throughout the class
    D. located at the two class boundaries

16. A fisherman decides that he needs a line that will test more than 10 pounds if he is to catch the size fish he desires.
He tests 16 pieces of Brand F line and finds a sample mean of 10.4. If it is known that the population standard deviation (G) = .5 pound, then the inference statement below that is CORRECT is   16.____

    A. Z = 3.2 and the chances are greater than 999 out of 1,000 that $\mu \geq 10$

    B. t = 3.2 and the chances are greater than 99 out of 100 that $\mu \geq 10$

    C. Z = .8 and the chances are only about 39 out of 100 that $\mu \geq 10$

    D. t = .8 and the chances are only 20 out of 100 that $\mu \geq 10$

17. A senior statistician in charge of a unit which requires the collection of statistical data from business on a regular basis recommends a method whereby small establishments report quarterly and the larger establishments are required to supply their information monthly. This recommended method applies BEST in circumstances where the burden of reporting is   17.____

A. geared to the ability of the business to supply the necessary information
B. shared among respondents so that no one business establishment carries a heavier burden than any other
C. partially borne by independent sources such as existing administrative records and the direct collection of information
D. not appreciably affected by reasonable estimations furnished when exact reported information is not supplied

18. Of the following, it is considered MOST likely that productivity will be GREATEST from a group of workers where the supervisor of the group

    18._____

A. acts as another employee among the group he supervises
B. is production-oriented primarily in his approach to supervision
C. uses the influence he has with his superiors to present employees' legitimate goals
D. receives emphasis on production from his superiors and, in turn, stresses production from his subordinates

19. Of the following, the basic intent of naming a form is to provide the means to

    19._____

A. code those factors recorded on each form
B. describe the use of the form
C. index each form
D. call attention to specific sections within each form

20. In the case where a major project is so complex that it is difficult to comprehend the entire scope of the work involved, it would be BEST in the planning and analysis of such a project to

    20._____

A. identify the common elements that are present in most statistical clerical operations
B. work out a series of checks in the major procedure to indicate any point in the procedure that is not functioning properly
C. present correlated activities graphically on charts and analyses
D. consider the entire project as made up of individual minor units

21. Good report writing utilizes, where possible, the use of table of contents, clear titles and subtitles, well-labeled tables and figures, and good summaries in prominent places. These features in a report are MOST helpful in

    21._____

A. saving the reader's time
B. emphasizing objectivity
C. providing a basic reference tool
D. forming a basis for future action

22. Of the following types of record forms used in an office, the one that is likely to be obsolete in a relatively short period of time and to require the greater control to prevent the accumulation of unnecessary data is the

    22._____

A. external transmittal record
B. internal transmittal record
C. journal record
D. report

23. Assume that you are a supervisor of staff. When your supervisor complains to you concerning a serious error on the part of one of your subordinates, the MOST proper response should be to

    A. state that you cannot do more than spotcheck the work of your subordinates
    B. accept the complaint and report the subordinate for disciplinary action
    C. tell your supervisor that you sincerely hope it will not happen again
    D. assure him that you will check on it to prevent a similar mistake in the future

    23.___

24. Of the following, the MOST practical way to lessen the problem of monotony in routine work is to

    A. rotate work assignments
    B. assign routine work to the less intelligent
    C. eliminate repetitive tasks
    D. get the subordinate to understand the importance of routine work

    24.___

25. The CHIEF value of organization charts for the supervisor or administrator is that they

    A. clarify and emphasize the informal but de factor shortcuts in inter-unit communication
    B. clearly outline the lines and levels of responsibility and supervision in the department
    C. prevent the misdirection of inter- and intra-departmental communication
    D. substantially reduce the amount of paper work

    25.___

KEY (CORRECT ANSWERS)

1.	A		11.	D
2.	B		12.	A
3.	A		13.	B
4.	A		14.	D
5.	C		15.	B
6.	B		16.	A
7.	B		17.	A
8.	A		18.	D
9.	D		19.	B
10.	B		20.	D

21.	A
22.	B
23.	D
24.	A
25.	B

SOLUTIONS TO PROBLEMS

1. CORRECT ANSWER: A
   In this fashion, only those respondents who actually had the equipment for automation would be used for further consideration. This procedure is more cost-effective than conducting library research. It is also more efficient time-wise.

2. CORRECT ANSWER: B
   Using the Poisson Distribution, $P(X=0) = 1^0 e^{-1} \div 0! = e^{-1} \approx .37$ (Recall $0! = 0$ factorial $= 1$)

3. CORRECT ANSWER: A
   $$r_{12.3} = [.3 - (.1)(.5)]/ \sqrt{(1-.01)(1-.25)}$$
   $$= .25/ \sqrt{.7425} \approx .29$$

4. CORRECT ANSWER: A
   It suffices to show that the numerators of the fractions representing each partial correlation coefficient is zero.

   For $r_{13.2}$, the corresponding numerator is $r_{13} - r_{12}r_{23} = p^2 - p.p = 0$. For $r_{14.2}$, the numerator is $r_{14} - r_{12}r_{24} = p^3 - p.p^2 = 0$. For $r_{24.3}$, the numerator is $r_{24} - r_{23}r_{34} = p^2 - p.p = 0$. Finally, for $r_{14.3}$, the numerator is $r_{14} - r_{13}r_{34} = p^3 - p^2.p = 0$.

5. CORRECT ANSWER: C
   The index of 100 is assigned to the average of the values of the months under consideration. If one particular month has an index of 120, we can be certain that at least one of the other months must have an index below 100.

6. CORRECT ANSWER: B
   Since the value of y is always positive, a must have a positive value. The value of b represents the slope, which is negative due to the fact that the series is declining over a period of time.

7. CORRECT ANSWER: B
   Although the Normal Distribution is widely used for many parametric formulas, such as the Poisson and Binomial formulas, it simply does not apply to data which are strictly random, or to non-parametric formulas.

8. CORRECT ANSWER: A
   In testing the hypothesis of whether r means are equal, we recognize that ANOVA techniques assume that these populations are normal with equal variances and that they are randomly drawn. ANOVA does NOT insist that each population has the same number of observations.

9. CORRECT ANSWER: D

With substitution, $R = \begin{vmatrix} 1 & .5 & -.5 \\ .5 & 1 & 0 \\ -.5 & 0 & 1 \end{vmatrix}$

$= (1)(1)(1) + (.5)(0)(-.5) + (-.5)(0)(.5) - (-.5)(1)(-.5) - (.5)(.5)(1) - (1)(0)(0) = .5$

$R_{11} = 1 - r^2_{23} = 1 - 0 = 1$

Thus, $R^2_{1.23} = 1 - .5/1 = 1/2$

10. CORRECT ANSWER: B
The expected values of the 4 cells would appear as:

	Few	Many
Small	48	12
Large	152	38

$x^2 = (50-48)^2/48 + (10-12)^2/12 + (150-152)^2/152 + (40-38)^2/38 \approx .548 \approx .55$

11. CORRECT ANSWER: D
A statistic (in this case, x) is considered a consistent estimator of a parameter (in this case, μ) if the probability that the value of x approaching the value of μ increases to 1 as the sample size approaches the population size.

12. CORRECT ANSWER: A
In a positively skewed distribution, the mode is less than the median and the median is less than the mean.

13. CORRECT ANSWER: B
Discriminant analysis generally attempts to classify any subjects being observed into two or more categories (populations) as a direct consequence of observations or measurements that are made. An example with 3 groups would be to identify a voter as Democrat, Republican, or Independent.

14. CORRECT ANSWER: D
By definition, chi-square represents distributions which are ratios of squared values, like $(n-1)s^2/\delta^2$, where n = sample size, δ^2 = population variance, δ^2 = sample variance. Another representation of chi-square would be $\Sigma (0_i - E_i)^2/E_i$, which is a summation of the squared values of differences between observed and expected frequencies divided by expected frequencies. Chi-square must always be non-negative.

15. CORRECT ANSWER: B
In the case of grouped data where a frequency curve has been constructed to fit the data, the mode will be the value (or values) of x corresponding to the maximum point or points on the curve. This value x is sometimes denoted by x .
From a frequency distribution or histogram, the mode can be obtained from the formula:

$$\text{Mode} = L_1 + \left(\frac{\Delta_1}{\Delta_1 + \Delta_2}\right)c$$

L_1 = lower class boundary of modal class (i.e., class containing the mode)

Δ_1 = excess of modal frequency over frequency of next lower class

Δ_2 = excess of modal frequency over frequency of next higher class

c = size of modal class interval.

This justifies answer B dispersed according to the frequencies in the two adjoining classes.

16. CORRECT ANSWER: A

Since the population standard deviation is known, we use the z-score test. $Z = (10.4 - 10)/(.5/\sqrt{16}) = 3.2$. Using the Normal Distribution Table of Z-scores, the probability that $\mu \geq 10$ is very close to .9993.

17. CORRECT ANSWER: A

As a rule, smaller businesses would not have the amount of resources as larger businesses in order to collect statistical data. Thus, the statistician would require the smaller businesses to submit data on a relatively infrequent basis (such as quarterly), whereas he would require the larger businesses to provide the needed data more frequently (such as monthly).

18. CORRECT ANSWER: D

The supervisor will attempt to show his workers that he (the supervisor) has been instructed from higher authority on the importance of production for the company. In this way, the supervised group will acquire a *team spirit* and thus maximize production.

19. CORRECT ANSWER: B

The form's name should be indicative of how the form will be used. Other considerations, like coding, would be secondary.

20. CORRECT ANSWER: D

By dividing up the project into smaller units, there is a much more realistic probability that each unit can be planned and analyzed. At a later stage, material connections can be formulated among several units.

21. CORRECT ANSWER: A

Usually a reader is interested in only a few topics of the report. A well-planned table of contents allows the reader to find those selected topics in a short time, without spending unnecessary time on other topics.

22. CORRECT ANSWER: B

This type of record may consist of very brief reminders or notes, and would be of little value after a period of time.

23. CORRECT ANSWER: D

This is the best course of action to take. Your supervisor needs to be assured that you will do whatever is humanly possible to prevent similar mistakes from re-occurring.

24. CORRECT ANSWER: A

This method affords each individual of performing different tasks within their capabilities.

25. CORRECT ANSWER: B

This describes exactly the purpose of organizational charts.

EXAMINATION SECTION
TEST 1

DIRECTIONS: Each question or incomplete statement is followed by several suggested answers or completions. Select the one that BEST answers the question or completes the statement. *PRINT THE LETTER OF THE CORRECT ANSWER IN THE SPACE AT THE RIGHT.*

1. If $m_x = D/P$, where m_x is the death rate, D is the number of deaths, P is the population; and if q_x, the probability of dying, equals $\dfrac{D}{P + \frac{1}{2}D}$, then the relationship between m_x and q_x is   1.____

   A. $q_x = \dfrac{2m_x}{2 + m_x}$ B. $q_x = \dfrac{m_x}{2 + m_x}$

   C. $m_x = \dfrac{2q_x}{2 + q_x}$ D. $m_x = \dfrac{q_x}{1 - q_x}$

2. In using the Chi-square technique for testing independence on data arranged in r rows and c columns, the number of degrees of freedom is equal to   2.____

   A. rc - 1   B. rc + 1
   C. r + c - 1   D. (r-1)(c-1)

3. If $(1 - R^2_{1.23}) = (1 - r^2_{13})(1 - r^2_{12.3})$ and $r_{13} = r_{12.3} = .5$, then $R_{1.23}$ equals   3.____

   A. .50   B. .56   C. .66   D. .86

4. The infinitely repeating decimal .148514851485... when converted to a fraction in its lowest reduced form is   4.____

   A. 165/1111   B. 15/101   C. 3/ 20   D. 1/ 7

5. In order to test the hypothesis that the variances -1^2 and -2^2 of two normally distributed populations are equal, based on two samples with n_1 and n_2 observations, we utilize the statistic   5.____

   A. $F = s_1^2/s_2^2$ and use the F-distribution table with n_1-1 and n_2-l degrees of freedom

   B. $F = s_1^2/s_2^2$ and use the F-distribution table with n_1 and n_2 degrees of freedom

   C. $X^2 = \dfrac{s_1^2 + s_2^2}{\sigma^2}$ with $n_1 + n_2$ degrees of freedom

   D. $F = \dfrac{n_1 s_1^2}{n_2 s_2^2}$ and use the F-distribution with n_1 and n_2 degrees of freedom

6. Answer this question on the basis of the information given in the table below. 6.___

Commodity	Unit	Quantity		Price Per Unit	
		2000	2005	2000	2005
Sugar	lb.	40	44	$1.20	$1.40
Flour	pkg.	80	85	$1.70	$1.90
Milk	qt.	25	20	$1.80	$2.20
Bread	loaf	15	20	$1.40	$1.60

The weighted aggregative (Laspeyres) price index for 2005 (2000 = 100) is

A. 114.6　　　　B. 114.7　　　　C. 114.8　　　　D. 114.9

7. The division of 110111 by 1011 in the binary scale gives the following result in the binary scale: 7.___

A. 101　　　　B. 110　　　　C. 111　　　　D. 1011

Questions 8-9.

DIRECTIONS: Questions 8 and 9 are to be answered on the basis of the information given below.

In the President's Manpower Report for 2004, a regression analysis was made of the percent change in Gross National Product (G) and Manufacturing Employment (M). The data used were as follows:

G	M
-2	-6.6
0	-4.0
2	-1.5
4	-1.0
6	3.5
8	6.0

(Calculations can be simplified by using deviation from the means.)

8. The regression equation based on the above data is 8.___

A. $M = -4.29 + 1.23G$
C. $G = -4.29 - 1.23M$
B. $M = -4.29 - 1.23G$
D. $G = 4.29 - 1.23M$

9. The correlation between G and M is 9.___

A. -.97　　　　B. -.98　　　　C. +.90　　　　D. +.98

10. The Housing Department wishes to make a study of the proportion of buildings that have violations. Assuming that a random sample is to be selected and that with 95 percent confidence a sampling error of 3 percent either way is permitted, how large a sample will be required? 10.___

A. 952　　　　B. 1067　　　　C. 1239　　　　D. 2347

11. Suppose there is a bakery that bakes cream cakes every morning. The cakes are such that unless sold every day, they have to be thrown away. For simplicity, assume the maximum number of customers a day is 3, and the maximum number of cakes baked a day is also 3. It costs $2 to bake a cake, and it is sold for $3. Assume that on 20 percent of the days, one customer comes in for a cake, that on 50 percent of the days 2 cakes would be sold, and that on 30 percent of the days 3 cakes would be sold. In order to MAXIMIZE his profits, how many cakes should the baker have on hand?

    A. 0   B. 1   C. 2   D. 3

12. A test to detect cancer is discovered that proves to be 95 percent reliable. If given to people who have cancer, the test will be positive 95 percent of the time and negative 5 percent of the time; if given to people who do not have cancer, the test will be negative 95 percent of the time and positive 5 percent of the time. Suppose this test is given to a large group of persons of whom 0.5 percent have cancer. Which of the following expresses MOST NEARLY the probability that a person with a positive test really has cancer?

    A. .95   B. .91   C. .09   D. .05

13. Answer this question on the basis of the table given below.

Age	PLANT A		PLANT B	
	Workers	Days Lost	Workers	Days Lost
20-29	100	600	400	2400
30-39	200	1600	400	3200
40-49	400	4000	100	1000
50+	400	4800	100	1200

In a study of absenteeism caused by sickness in two different plants, the average days lost were 10 per man in Plant A and 7.8 per man in Plant B. Upon further analysis of the data above on which these averages were based, the statistician concluded that

    A. standardizing the rates by age group results in no difference in the averages
    B. the difference is not statistically significant
    C. in addition to the averages, the variations in the data should be presented
    D. A X^2 test should be used to determine the significance of the differences

14. One version of the Law of Large Numbers states that

$$P[(M\text{-}m) \leq \frac{KS}{\sqrt{n}}] = \frac{1}{K^2}$$

Using this fact, how large a sample (n) is needed at the 5 percent significance level so that the sample mean (m) will be within s/2 of the universe mean (M)?

    A. 160   B. 80   C. 20   D. 5

15. Seventy percent of the firms in a large trade association made a profit last year. The probability that in a simple random sample of 3 firms, exactly 2 out of 3 firms will make a profit is

    A. .33   B. .44   C. .56   D. .67

16. If all samples consisting of two numbers are selected from the population consisting of the numbers 2, 4, 8, 10, then the sum of the mean and variance of the resulting sampling distribution is

    A. 6.8   B. 7.8   C. 9.3   D. 11.0

16.____

17. If we add a constant to each observation in a regression problem, $y = a + bx$, we

    A. do not change the correlation coefficient
    B. change the regression coefficient, b
    C. do not change the value of any part of the regression equation
    D. do not change the value of the constant term, a

17.____

18. Heights of army men are normally distributed with a mean of 68 inches and a standard deviation of 3 inches.
The percent of this population between 65 and 74 inches is MOST NEARLY

    A. 90%   B. 82%   C. 68%   D. 62%

18.____

19. As a statistician on a project, you have been assigned to design a punch card. You find that you need 82 columns for your data, but have only 80 columns on the card. You observe that you have assigned three columns to dichotomous data of the yes-no type. The BEST way to solve this dilemma is to

    A. punch the additional two columns on another card since the format for reading the data can easily be adjusted
    B. use a 1-column code for the three columns of dichotomous data based on the binary number system
    C. utilize the X and Y punches on the card
    D. utilize an alphabetic code

19.____

20. In testing hypotheses, the probability of a Type 1 error can be made smaller either by increasing the sample size, or by

    A. increasing the Type II error
    B. subtracting Yates' correction factor
    C. utilizing Fisher's z distribution
    D. using a nonparametric test

20.____

KEY (CORRECT ANSWERS)

1.	A		11.	C
2.	D		12.	C
3.	C		13.	A
4.	B		14.	B
5.	A		15.	B
6.	C		16.	D
7.	A		17.	A
8.	A		18.	B
9.	D		19.	B
10.	B		20.	A

———

SOLUTIONS TO PROBLEMS

1. CORRECT ANSWER: A

   $q_x = D/(p + 1/2D) = 2D/(2P+D)$

   $\quad = 2Pm_x/(2P+Pm_x$

   $\quad = 2Pm_x/[P(2+m_x)] = 2m_x/(2+m_x)$

2. CORRECT ANSWER: D

   With r rows and c columns, $(r-1)(c-1)$ equals the degrees of freedom.

3. CORRECT ANSWER: C

   $(1-R^2_{1.23}) = (1-.5^2)(1-.5^2) = .75^2 = .5625$

   Then, $R^2 1.23 = .4375$ and $R_{1.23} \approx .66$

4. CORRECT ANSWER: B

   Let $N = \overline{.1485}$, so that $10{,}000N = 1485.\overline{1485}$

   By subtraction, $9999N = 1485$, and $N = 1485/9999$.

   In lowest terms, $N = 15/101$

5. CORRECT ANSWER: A

   This test assumes independence of samples. Also, s_1^2 should always be the larger variance.

6. CORRECT ANSWER: C

   The base year 2000 calculations $(40)(1.20) + (80)(1.70) +$
   $(25)(1.80) + (15)(1.40) = 250.00$
   The 2005 year calculation =

   $(\frac{140}{120})(40)(1.20) + (\frac{190}{170})(80)(1.70) + (\frac{220}{180})(25)(1.80) + (\frac{160}{140})(15)(1.40)$
   $= 287.00$

   The Laspeyres price index $= \frac{287.00}{250.00} \times 100 = 114.8$

7. CORRECT ANSWER: A

   $110111_{base\ 2} = 32 + 16 + 4 + 2 + 1 = 55_{base\ 10}$

   $1011_{base\ 2} = 8 + 2 + 1 + = 11_{base\ 10}$

   $55/11 = 5 = 101_{base\ 2}$

8. CORRECT ANSWER: A

   The regression equation is found by solving the following

   equations: $\sum = 6a + b\sum G$ and $\sum MG = a\sum G + b\sum G^2$. These
   become: $-3.6 = 6a + 18b$ and $75.2 = 18a + 124b$. Solving,
   $a = -4.28$ and $b = 1.23$

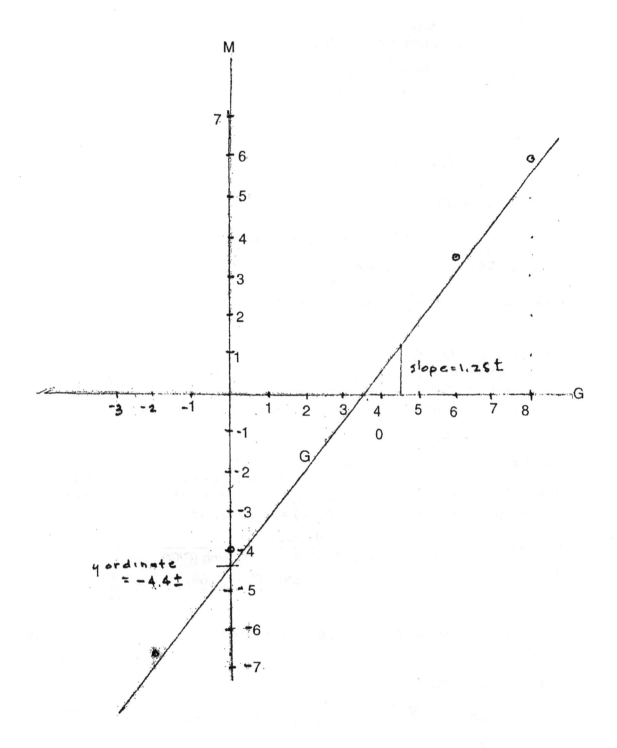

slope=1.25 ±

y ordinate
= -4.4 ±

9. CORRECT ANSWER: D

The correlation coefficient, r, is given by:

$$r = \frac{6(\Sigma MG) - (\Sigma M)(\Sigma G)}{\sqrt{[6(\Sigma M^2) - (\Sigma M)^2] \cdot [6(\Sigma G^2) - (\Sigma G)^2]}}$$

$$= \frac{6(75.2) - (18)(-3.6)}{\sqrt{[6(111.06) - (-3.6)^2] \cdot [6(124) - (18)^2]}}$$

$$= 516/\sqrt{(653.4)(420)} \approx +.98$$

10. CORRECT ANSWER: B

The formula is: $n = \hat{p}\hat{q}(\frac{Z_{\alpha/2}}{E})^2$. Since $\hat{p}, \hat{q}$ are unknown, use a value of .5 for each. E = .03 and $Z_{\alpha/2} = Z_{.025} = 1.96$

Then, $n = (.5)(.5)(\frac{1.96}{.03})^2 = 1067.\overline{1} \approx 1067$

11. CORRECT ANSWER: C

Eliminate choice A. By baking 1 cake, his expected profit = (1)(.20) + (1)(.5) + (1)(.3) = $1. By baking 2 cakes, the expected profit = (-1)(.2) + (2)(.5) + (2)(.3) = $1.40. Finally, baking 3 cakes, the profit = (-3)(.2) + (0)(.5) + (3)(.3) = $0.30. He should bake 2 cakes.

12. CORRECT ANSWER: C

This is a classic Buyes' Theorem application.

Let P = tests positive, C = has cancer, C' = does not have cancer, and N = tests negative. Prob (P|C) = .95, Prob (N|C) = .05, Prob (N|C') = .95, Prob (P|C'). = .05. We seek the value of Prob (C|P). We also know Prob (C) = .005 and Prob (C') = .995.

Now Prob (C P) = $\dfrac{\text{Prob (C)} \cdot \text{Prob (P/C)}}{\text{Prob(C)} \cdot \text{Prob (P|C)} + \text{Prob (C')} \cdot \text{Prob (P/C')}}$

= (.005)(.95)/[(.005)(.95)+(.995)(.05)] $\approx$ .09

13. CORRECT ANSWER: A

For both plants, the rates of days lost per worker in the four age groups are: 6, 8, 10, and 12, respectively.

14. CORRECT ANSWER: B

Since $\frac{1}{k^2} = .05$, $k = \sqrt{20}$. . Now, since $ks/\sqrt{n} = s/2$ in this example, we get $\sqrt{20}./\sqrt{n} = \frac{1}{2}$ (s's cancel). Solving, n = 80.

15. CORRECT ANSWER: B

The probability is given by $(_3C_2)(.70)^2(.30)^1 = .441 \approx .44$

16. CORRECT ANSWER: D

The mean, μ, of this population is $(2+4+8+10)/4 = 6$ and its standard deviation, δ, is

given by $\sqrt{[(2\text{-}6)^2 + (4\text{-}6)^2 + (8\text{-}6)^2 + (10\text{-}6)^2]/4} = \sqrt{10}$.

For all samples of size taken from this population, the mean, μ_x, is 6 and the standard

deviation, $\delta_x = \sqrt{10}/\sqrt{2} \approx 2.236$ so δ_x^2 (variance) = 5. Then, $\mu_x + \delta_x^2 = 11.0$

17. CORRECT ANSWER: A

The only effect of adding a constant to each of the observations
is that the y-intercept a will be altered by that constant.
The b value of $y = a + bx$ and the correlation coefficient remain the same.

18. CORRECT ANSWER: B

Change 65 and 74 to z scores: 65 becomes $(65\text{-}68)/3 = -1$
and 74 becomes $(74\text{-}68)/3 = 2$.
Prob $(-1 < z < 2)$ in a Normal Distribution = .3413 + .4772 =
$.8185 \approx 82\%$

19. CORRECT ANSWER: B

The 1-column code would be a number from 0 through 7.
Suppose 0 = yes, 1 = no. The original 3 columns would read as a triple, such as 101.
Simply convert this, using the binary system, to a digit from 0 to 7. In this instance, 101
would be 5.

20. CORRECT ANSWER: A

The Type II error denotes accepting a false hypothesis. By increasing this error, we can
reduce the Type I error, which signifies rejecting a true hypothesis.

TEST 2

DIRECTIONS: Each question or incomplete statement is followed by several suggested answers or completions. Select the one that BEST answers the question or completes the statement. *PRINT THE LETTER OF THE CORRECT ANSWER IN THE SPACE AT THE RIGHT.*

1. Which BEST describes the method to use in fitting a curve to the data on the population of New York City for the decades from 1790 through 1970?   1.____

   A. Logistic   B. Straight line
   C. Gompertz curve   D. Parabola

2. Government statistical work can either be organized into one statistical agency that ser-   2.____
   vices all departments or into separate statistical units in each department.
   The MAJOR advantage of a central agency is that

   A. one giant computer can service the data needs of all departments
   B. it is more sensitive and responsive to data needs for policy-making
   C. it overcomes the defects of overproliferation of statistical operations
   D. economies of scale lead to less efficiency and the application of greater expertise

3. In many multi-purpose surveys of the characteristics of individuals, some people refuse   3.____
   to report their wage or income data.
   The BEST way to overcome this deficiency is to

   A. get the respondent to answer by threatening to jail or fine him
   B. impute the missing data by having the computer assign the same data for this
      report as the next report with identical characteristics on other measured variables
   C. look up his income tax record and use the data from this source
   D. leave the columns blank on the punch card and leave such reports out of wage or
      income tabulations until later research establishes the clarity of such matters

4. The BEST way in which to derive morbidity statistics for all sickness, major and minor,   4.____
   experienced by a population is to

   A. secure the records of a representative sample of industrial establishments on sick-
      ness absenteeism
   B. conduct a study of the illnesses and characteristics of hospital in-patients
   C. conduct a study of visits and consultations in stratified samples of general practitio-
      ners
   D. conduct a sample survey of the population, and ask them what sickness they had
      during the last month

5. The point of intersection of the *less than* and *more than* cumulative frequency curves is   5.____
   always at the

   A. arithmetic mean in a bivariate sample
   B. geometric mean in any sample
   C. harmonic mean in a skewed sample
   D. median, whether the sample is skewed or normal

6. In some ways time series analysis is the least satisfying area of statistical analysis from the theoretical viewpoint.
   This statement refers to the fact that

    A. exact data needed for time series analysis are difficult to obtain
    B. time series computations are complex
    C. time series observations are not random drawings from a population
    D. time series represent bivariate data

6._____

7. The use of moving averages on a time series will

    A. eliminate bias
    B. make possible predictions of values beyond the range of the original data
    C. provide a mathematical expression for the underlying curve
    D. reveal the general trend

7._____

8. Sequential sampling designs should be used when

    A. a decision must be reached in a specified short time
    B. each observation is expensive to get
    C. many test cases are easily available
    D. uniformity of tests is essential

8._____

9. As a statistician with no knowledge of computer technology, you have been assigned to be liaison with the computer division on a mass project.
   Your PRIMARY function should be to

    A. review the programming steps to insure accuracy of the program
    B. indicate to the computer section what the statistical input and desired analytic output will be
    C. follow each important step in the processing of the data
    D. devote your time to setting up the input and leave the form of the output to the computer section

9._____

10. In comparing parametric with nonparametric methods, the following statement is TRUE: Nonparametric

    A. methods generally require larger samples at the same level of significance
    B. tests use all the information available in sampled data
    C. methods always require larger samples at the same level of significance
    D. statistics are harder to compute

10._____

11. A skin specialist reported that adolescent acne (pimples) are twice as common in females as in males. He based this conclusion on an enumeration of all his patients. This is a FAULTY conclusion because

    A. such a result could have been obtained simply by chance
    B. from a statistical and research design point of view, he did not consider the sampling errors of his study
    C. he would have obtained more representative results if he had sampled his patients in accordance with other outside variables
    D. adolescent girls are more likely than boys to be concerned about their appearance and hence are more apt to visit a skin specialist

11._____

12. A community has been making population estimates by the cohort method, utilizing   12.____
births, deaths, and the school census as a measure of net migration. The results of the
census seemed to indicate that the population estimate grossly overstated the population. As a statistician, you have been assigned to look into the apparent discrepancy.
You should

    A. recommend that the community pay for a new census because you believe that
important population groups in your community were undercounted
    B. state that the census as the official count is right and that the estimates were
wrong
    C. make a careful analysis of the differences by age, sex, and race to determine the
extent and reasons for the differences in the known elements
    D. declare that the census results are wrong since they disagree with the known data

13. The coding of industry and occupation is one of the more difficult parts of the census of   13.____
population's coding structure.
In order to check on the accuracy of this coding, you should

    A. machine edit all coding and not rehire workers with too many errors
    B. sample each coder's work and dismiss those who don't meet standards
    C. check all coding 100 percent, and reassign coders who do not meet quality stan-
dards
    D. select a sample of each coder's work and, if quality standards are not met, shift the
coder to other work

14. In determining whether a sample could have come from a certain universe, we could use   14.____
either the X^2 test of goodness of fit or the much simpler

    A. Kolmogorov-Smirnov test
    B. Spearman's rank correlation
    C. Mann-Whitney test
    D. Kruskal-Wallis test

15. The criterion that a point estimator from a sample has the lowest variance among all   15.____
other point estimators of the population parameter is called

    A. unbiasedness   B. sufficiency
    C. consistency   D. efficiency

16. In stratified sampling, it is desirable that each stratum be   16.____

    A. equal in size   B. homoscedastic
    C. heterogeneous   D. homogeneous

17. A basic characteristic that distinguishes an electronic computer (EDP) system from the   17.____
old punch card system (E.A.M.) is the

    A. use of punched card input
    B. ability to get printed output
    C. use of a programmed sequence of operations
    D. use of numeric codes to represent data

18. A statistician gave a series of multiple regression problems, with a large number of variables, to three different computer centers and received three different sets of equations. This kind of mistake is MOST likely to be caused by

    A. differences in rounding procedures used at the computer centers
    B. mistakes in programming since the programs are not likely to be checked among the installations
    C. differential bugs in compilers of different computers
    D. the fact that computers cannot solve large numbers of simultaneous equations

18.____

19. Of the following, the BEST way to detect partisan treatment of data in a statistical study is to

    A. reject the conclusions stated if you do not agree with them
    B. check the conclusions wherever possible by independent investigation
    C. remember that a statement in print provides no statement of reliability
    D. present contradictory evidence, even if unsubstantiated, and observe the reaction

19.____

20. In a recent study of existing health insurance, a small but significant proportion of respondents reported that they had *loss of income protection* under Blue Shield. This was wrong since Blue Shield does not provide such benefits. This type of response error is

    A. balanced by other types of errors
    B. corrected by taking larger samples
    C. not possible to detect by editing techniques
    D. not taken into account by the sampling error formulas

20.____

KEY (CORRECT ANSWERS)

1.	A		11.	D
2.	C		12.	C
3.	B		13.	D
4.	D		14.	A
5.	D		15.	D
6.	C		16.	D
7.	D		17.	C
8.	B		18.	A
9.	B		19.	B
10.	A		20.	D

SOLUTIONS TO PROBLEMS

1. CORRECT ANSWER: A
    Logistic equations are best used to describe population growth.
    skt A typical equation is $y = S/[1+Ce^{-skt}]$, where y = population at time t, S = maximum population, K = constant, and C = (s-yo)/yo with yo = initial population.

2. CORRECT ANSWER: C
    By having separate units, there would be a tendency for each unit to perform statistical operations, even unnecessarily. The results of these operations then would be difficult to summarize, lacking a central agency.

3. CORRECT ANSWER: B
    Statisticians need to report all data. If a particular variable (wages, other income) is not available for all respondents, the missing data is best replaced by whatever was reported on the next respondent with identical (or very similar) characteristics.

4. CORRECT ANSWER: D
    By conducting a random sample survey, we get a better picture on various morbidity statistics. This is certainly preferable to going to hospitals or to doctors, since we will probably <u>only</u> get data on <u>major</u> sicknesses.

5. CORRECT ANSWER: D
    The median represents the value where exactly one-half of the distribution lies below it and one-half lies above it. Thus, 50% of the values are less than the median and 50% of the values are more than the median.

6. CORRECT ANSWER: C
    Time series involves observations taken at <u>specific</u> intervals, such as each month or each year. In the theoretical sense, statistical formulas and models are based on randomness of events. This is absent from time series analyses.

7. CORRECT ANSWER: D
    A moving average would detect changes in data, large or small. For example, a 3-month moving average would first take the average values of January, February, and March; then the average of February, March, and April, etc. The change in averages would be revealed, and this would indicate any trend.

8. CORRECT ANSWER: C
    Sequential sampling provides for taking as many samples as necessary in order to reach a decision concerning acceptance or rejection of a product. This is possible when many test cases are available (and cost is not a major issue).

9. CORRECT ANSWER: B
    The computer division will be then able to design its program(s) to function so that the statistician can interpret the resulting output correctly.

10. CORRECT ANSWER: A
Non-parametric methods do not require any assumptions concerning the population from which samples are drawn. Their computations are also generally easier than those for parametric methods. As a result, larger samples are needed to attain the same level of significance when a parametric method is used.

11. CORRECT ANSWER: D
Since the skin specialist would examine considerably more females than males, his conclusion about the frequency of acne in girls vs. boys would be faulty.

12. CORRECT ANSWER: C
The statistician needs to examine specific categories which are readily definable, such as age and sex. The errors in the estimate can then be traced to one or more of these defined categories.

13. CORRECT ANSWER: D
To maximize efficiency and accuracy, assign only the best coders to the coding assignment. The other workers would be better suited to an easier task.

14. CORRECT ANSWER: A
This test converts frequencies (observed) to cumulative frequencies and then cumulative proportions are found. Using cumulative proportions of both observed and expected frequencies, the actual test involves comparing D, which is the <u>largest</u> difference between observed and expected frequencies (cumulative). This test is superior to the X^2 test, when the distribution is not normal.

15. CORRECT ANSWER: D
The efficiency of any statistic is measured by the size of its standard error or variance. Since a point estimator has the lowest variance, when drawn from a sample, it has the highest efficiency in the measurement of the corresponding population parameter.

16. CORRECT ANSWER: D
In stratified sampling, we attempt to provide that various homogeneous subgroups are represented in the sample in accordance with their respective representation in the population.

17. CORRECT ANSWER: C
All computer systems use programmable operations and calculations.

18. CORRECT ANSWER: A
Each computer center's capability to identify the exactness of the regression coefficients will differ slightly due to rounding in the calculations.

19. CORRECT ANSWER: B
Self-explanatory.

20. CORRECT ANSWER: D
In this scenario, the respondents did not understand the meaning of *loss of income protection*. The sampling error formulas cannot detect this mistake.

EXAMINATION SECTION
TEST 1

DIRECTIONS: Each question or incomplete statement is followed by several suggested answers or completions. Select the one that BEST answers the question or completes the statement. *PRINT THE LETTER OF THE CORRECT ANSWER IN THE SPACE AT THE RIGHT.*

1. The one of the following which is NOT a measure of the spread or variability of a distribution is the _____ deviation.

   1.____

   A.   mean   B.   orthogonal   C.   quartile   D.   standard

2. The one of the following which is NOT a probability or frequency distribution is a _____ distribution.

   2.____

   A.   rectangular   B.   binomial   C.   hypergeometric   D.   circular

3. The mean is always equal to the variance in a _____ distribution.

   3.____

   A.   Poisson   B.   rectangular   C.   Lexian   D.   Cauchy

4. In a certain large office, 40 percent of the employees are women.
    If a sample of five employees is selected at random, the probability that exactly two of the five are women is MOST NEARLY

   4.____

   A.   .45   B.   .35   C.   .20   D.   .15

5. The coefficient of variation is a useful measure of relative variability when

   5.____

   A.   two variables with different units of measure are to be compared
   B.   two variables are correlated
   C.   two variables are normally distributed
   D.   a qualitative variable is compared with a measurable variable

6. A stationary time series is a series which has no

   6.____

   A.   autocorrelation   B.   cyclical movement
   C.   variance   D.   trend

7. A hundred observations on a certain variable X are obtained and found to have variance equal to 2. Suppose that every observation is multiplied by 2.
    The hundred observations on the new variable $Y = 2X$ have variance equal to

   7.____

   A.   3   B.   5   C.   7   D.   8

Questions 8-9.

DIRECTIONS: Questions 8 and 9 are to be answered on the basis of the following data.

The following distribution of workers in a certain country by annual income class was obtained:

Annual Income Class	Fraction of All Workers
1 (lowest income group)	.35
2	.40
3	.13
4	.09
5 (highest income group)	.03
Total	1.00

8. If two workers are selected at random, the probability that one will belong to class 2 and the other will belong to class 4 is MOST NEARLY   8.___

    A. 30.6   B. 3.6   C. .36   D. .036

9. If a single worker is selected at random, the probability that he will belong to either class 1 or class 5 is MOST NEARLY   9.___

    A. .57   B. .38   C. .234   D. .0212

10. If the value of a statistic approaches more and more closely the estimated parameter as the sample size is indefinitely increased, it is called   10.___

    A. consistent   B. valid
    C. sufficient   D. reliable

11. The limiting form of the binomial distribution as P becomes very small is the _____ dis-   11.___
tribution.

    A. anomalous   B. Cauchy
    C. Poisson   D. Chi-square

12. The distribution of means of samples from any population, as the size of the sample is increased, tends toward the _____ distribution.   12.___

    A. reticular   B. Poisson
    C. normal   D. binomial

Questions 13-15.

DIRECTIONS: Questions 13 through 15 are to be answered on the basis of the following data.

100 trials of an experiment are conducted in which the proba-bility of a *success* on any single trial is .2. Let X be the number of successes obtained in the 100 trials.

13. The average (expected) value of X in repeated sets of 100 trials is   13.___

    A. 15   B. 20   C. 25   D. 35

14. The variance of X in repeated sets of 100 trials is   14.___

    A. 2   B. 6   C. 16   D. 32

15. The variance of X/100 in repeated sets of 100 trials is   15.___

Questions 16-18.

DIRECTIONS: Questions 16 through 18 are to be answered on the basis of the following table.

95 Percent Confidence Interval for Binomial Distribution

Fraction of successes observed x/n	Size of Sample					
	100		250		1,000	
.15	.09	.24	.10	.20	.13	.17
.25	.17	.35	.20	.31	.22	.28
.35	.26	.45	.29	.41	.32	.38

16. In a sample of 100 cases, the fraction of successes observed, x/n , is .25.   16._____
Using the above table, the one of the following hypotheses which should be accepted
is that P

    A.   is less than .14   B.   is more than .34
    C.   is less than .38   D.   = .35

17. If the sample totaled 250 cases and x/n = .15, the one of the following hypotheses which   17._____
should be rejected is that P is

    A.   .13   B.   .15   C.   .19   D.   .22

18. A random sample of individuals is checked for an attribute, and 95 percent confidence   18._____
limits for the fraction of individuals in the population having the attribute are obtained
from tables like the one above.
The limits obtained are such that

    A.   95 percent of the individuals lie within the limits
    B.   95 percent of future sample fractions will lie within these limits
    C.   the probability that the population fraction lies within these limits is .95
    D.   if we always obtain our limits in this way, then they will include the population frac-
        tion 95 percent of the time

19. The hypothesis that no true difference exists between two samples, that in fact these   19._____
samples were randomly drawn from the same population and differ only by accidents of
sampling, is called the _____ hypothesis.

    A.   null   B.   collateral
    C.   Tchebycheff   D.   Neyman-Pearson

20. If H_0 is the given hypothesis and H_1 is the alternative hypothesis, an error of Type I is   20._____
made when

    A. H_1 is rejected although it is in fact the correct hypothesis
    B. H_0 is accepted although it is in fact the incorrect hypothesis
    C. H_0 is rejected although it is in fact the correct hypothesis
    D. H_0 is accepted as not being significantly different from H_1 although it is in fact dif-
        ferent

21. If H_0 is the given hypothesis and H_1 is the alternative hypothesis, the power of the critical   21._____
region R with respect to the alternative hypothesis H_1 is equal to

    A.   1 minus the probability of making an error of Type II
    B.   the probability of making an error of Type I
    C.   1 minus the probability of making an error of Type III
    D.   the probability of making an error of Type II

22. In testing the significance of differences between percentages, the distribution to be used is the _____ distribution.

    A.   normal
    C.   rectangular
    B.   hypergeometric
    D.   Lorian

22.___

23. In using the chi-square formula for testing agreement between observed and expected results, if the data are tabulated in r rows and c columns, the number of degrees of freedom is equal to

    A.   rc + 1r
    C.   (r+c)(r-c)
    B.   (r-1)(c-1)
    D.   rc - 1c

23.___

24. In testing whether a regression coefficient is signifi-cantly different from zero, the distribution to be used is the _____ distribution.

    A.   Cauchy
    C.   Poisson
    B.   catastrophic
    D.   t-

24.___

25. *In 176 years, the Lower Mississippi River has shortened itself 242 miles. Therefore, a million years ago, the Lower Mississippi River was 1,300,000 miles long.*
This is an example of an unwarranted use of

    A.   correlative regression
    C.   extrapolation
    B.   linear regression
    D.   curvilinear interpolation

25.___

26. The correlation coefficient is usually spoken of as a measure of the strength of the linear relationship between two

    A.   means
    C.   parameters
    B.   modes
    D.   variables

26.___

27. No assumption about the normality of the population distribution is necessary when one uses

    A.   analysis of compatibility
    B.   multiple correlation
    C.   partial correlation
    D.   rank correlationRT

27.___

28. The linear function of the observations which will dis-tinguish better than any other linear function between the two groups on which common measurements are available is called a _____ function.

    A.   regression
    C.   least squares
    B.   discriminant
    D.   concentric

28.___

29. A statistical association between two variables may be evidence of a real association according to various tests and measurements of the regression analysis, but statis-tical association can in no way imply

    A.   variation
    C.   correlation
    B.   causation
    D.   integration

29.___

30. A fairly regular oscillation in a time series within each year which occurs regardless of the general trend or the position of the cyclical movement is called a(n)   30.____

    A.   autocorrelation   B.   slant correlation
    C.   seasonal variation   D.   variate difference

31. Given a least squares regression line of y on x: $y = .4 + .12x$, where x is the yearly income (in thousands of dollars) and y is the monthly food bill (in hundreds of dollars). If a family has a yearly income of $7,000, the predicted monthly expenditure for food is MOST NEARLY   31.____

    A. $96   B. $124   C. $184   D. $216

32. For a certain group of persons, the correlation between average grades in college and earnings ten years after graduation is found to be .64.
The percentage of the variability in earnings which is explainable by differences in college grades is MOST NEARLY _____ percent.   32.____

    A.   72   B.   68   C.   41   D.   32

33. The regression equation for y on x may be written as: $y - \bar{y} = r(\frac{\sigma y}{\sigma x})(x - \bar{x})$ The regression equation for x on y when $\bar{x} = 3$, $\bar{y} = 6$, $\sigma x = 2$, $\sigma y = 3$ and $r = .6$ is   33.____

    A. $5x = 2y + 3$ B. $5x = 3y - 16$
    C. $x = 2y - 12$ D. $x = y - 16$

34. The number of different samples of three elements that can be drawn from a finite population of six elements is equal to   34.____

    A.   16   B.   19   C.   20   D.   23

35. As far as possible, in cluster sampling, each cluster, within itself, should be   35.____

    A.   normally distributed   B.   consistent
    C.   heterogeneous   D.   homogeneous

36. In sample surveys, failure to reach all respondents, poor reliability and validity of responses, and faulty interpretation of data are regarded as   36.____

    A.   part of the random sampling variance
    B.   part of the non-sampling errors
    C.   part of the systematic variances
    D.   nugatory since they tend to cancel each other.

37. Systematic sampling is LEAST likely to be similar to _____ sampling.   37.____

    A.   simple random   B.   cluster
    C.   stratified random   D.   quota

38. In stratified random sampling,   38.____

    A.   a sample of selected strata is used
    B.   a sample is selected from each stratum
    C.   every K-th item is selected for the sample
    D.   each stratum should be heterogeneous

39. If the sample size is doubled, the variance of the sampling distribution of the mean is multiplied by

39.____

   A. 3   B. 1   C. /3   D. 1/2

40. If random samples of size n are drawn from a specified population in order to estimate the proportion, P, of individuals possessing a certain characteristic, the sample proportion, P, of individuals possessing this characteristic can be used as an estimate of P.

40.____

The variance of P' is $\dfrac{(N-n)}{(n-1)} \cdot \dfrac{P(1-P)}{n}$, where N is the total size of the population.

The quantity $\dfrac{N-n}{N-1}$ is frequently referred to as

   A.   Sheppard's correction
   B.   correction factor for finite population
   C.   correction factor for degrees of freedom
   D.   correction factor for elasticity

———

KEY (CORRECT ANSWERS)

1. B	11. C	21. A	31. B
2. D	12. C	22. A	32. C
3. A	13. B	23. B	33. A
4. B	14. C	24. D	34. C
5. A	15. A	25. C	35. C
6. D	16. C	26. D	36. B
7. D	17. D	27. D	37. D
8. D	18. D	28. B	38. B
9. B	19. A	29. B	39. D
10. A	20. C	30. C	40. B

SOLUTIONS TO PROBLEMS

1. CORRECT ANSWER: B
Orthogonal deviations are fictitious. Deviations can be mean, quartile, or standard.

2. CORRECT ANSWER: D
No distribution can be described as circular. Rectangular, binomial, and hypergeometric can be used to describe a frequency distribution.

3. CORRECT ANSWER: A
The formula can be written as $P(X-x)=e^{-\lambda} \cdot \lambda^x /x!$ for $x = 0,1,2,..., \lambda > 0$. The mean = the variance = λ.

4. CORRECT ANSWER: B
The probability = $(_5C_2)(.40)^2(.60)^3 = .3456 \approx .35$

5. CORRECT ANSWER: A
The coefficient of variation = $(\sigma/\mu) \cdot 100$ where σ = standard deviation and μ = mean.

6. CORRECT ANSWER: D
A trend is a pattern which shows growth or a decrease over time, which stationary series lack.

7. CORRECT ANSWER: D
If each observation is multiplied by 2, the original variance is multiplied by $2^2 = 4$. Since the original variance was 2, the new variance = $(2)(4) = 8$

8. CORRECT ANSWER: D
The required probability = $(.40)(.09) = .036$.

9. CORRECT ANSWER: B
The probability = $.35 + .03 = .38$

10. CORRECT ANSWER: A
A statistic is consistent if: as the sample size is increased, the statistic approaches the population parameter.

11. CORRECT ANSWER: C
If, in a binomial distribution, the number of trials (n) exceeds 30 and $p < .05$, the Poisson distribution can be used as a good approximation. In this case, replace A by np as the mean.

12. CORRECT ANSWER: C
The distribution of sample means approaches a normal distribution as the sample size increases. The mean of this distribution = the mean of the original population.

13. CORRECT ANSWER: B
The expected value of $x = (.2)(100) = 20$

14. CORRECT ANSWER: C
The variance of $x = (.2)(.8)(100) = 16$

15. CORRECT ANSWER: A

The variance of $\frac{1}{100}x = (\text{variance of } x)(\frac{1}{100})^2 = (16)(\frac{1}{10,000}) = .0016$

16. CORRECT ANSWER: C

The chart shows a 95% probability that the value of p lies between .17 and .35.

17. CORRECT ANSWER: D

The chart shows a 95% probability that the value of p lies between .10 and .20. Thus, reject p = .22

18. CORRECT ANSWER: D

By selecting different samples of the same size from the population, we obtain different intervals to capture the value of y. Then 95% of these intervals will actually contain the value of y.

19. CORRECT ANSWER: A

A null hypothesis would assume no actual statistical difference exists between two given samples.

20. CORRECT ANSWER: C

By definition, this is an error of Type I.

21. CORRECT ANSWER: A

The power is $1 - \beta$, where β is the probability of accepting the alternative hypothesis (H_1) when it is false.

22. CORRECT ANSWER: A

In testing the differences between percentages, the normal distribution is applied by

converting to a $z = \dfrac{p_1 - p_2}{\sqrt{\bar{p}\,\bar{q}(\frac{1}{n_1} + \frac{1}{n_2})}}$ Here, p_1 and p_2 represent the sample percents (or

proportions), n_1, n_2 are the sample sizes, $\bar{p}$ is the pooled percent and $\bar{q} = 1 - \bar{p}$

23. CORRECT ANSWER: B

In chi-square tests for observed and expected values, the degrees of freedom = (r-1)(c-1), where r = number of rows, c = number of columns.

24. CORRECT ANSWER: D

To test the significance of a regression coefficient, β, we would use $t_{n-k-1} = \dfrac{b}{s_b}$, where

b = sample statistic used to sb measure β, n-k-1 = degrees of freedom, sb = standard error

25. CORRECT ANSWER: C

Predictive data should only be used for reasonably-sized data values.

26. CORRECT ANSWER: D

A correlation coefficient measures the linear relationship between 2 variables.

27. CORRECT ANSWER: D
Rank correlation tests concerning populations are non-parametric. They don't depend on a normal population.

28. CORRECT ANSWER: B
By definition.

29. CORRECT ANSWER: B
A statistical association indicates the strength of the relation-ship between the two variables. However, we cannot say that one variable's change causes the other variable's change.

30. CORRECT ANSWER: C
For each year, the same oscillation occurs at the same time of the time series.

31. CORRECT ANSWER: B
Substitute so that y = .4 + (.12)(7) = 1.24 hundreds of dollars = $124.

32. CORRECT ANSWER: C
The percentage of variability = $(correlation)^2 = (.64)^2 = .41$

33. CORRECT ANSWER: A
The equation will be $x - \bar{x} = (t)(\frac{\sigma x}{\sigma y})(y - \bar{y})$. Then, x - 3 = $(.6)(\frac{2}{3})(y - 6)$. This simplifies to

$x - 3 = \frac{2}{5}(y - 6)$. Finally, 5x - 15 = 2y - 12 or 5x = 2y + 3

34. CORRECT ANSWER: C
The number of samples = $_6C_3$ = [(6)(5)(4)]/[(3)(2)(1)] = 120/6 = 20

35. CORRECT ANSWER: C
The original population is subdivided into clusters. Each cluster sampled should represent a *mix* of values.

36. CORRECT ANSWER: B
These are errors arising from external factors unrelated to the actual sampling process.

37. CORRECT ANSWER: D
In systemic sampling, a particular entity (e.g., a name in a phone book) would be selected. Then, every 10th name after this name would be chosen. Quota sampling would seek repre-sentative names of different origins.

38. CORRECT ANSWER: B
This is the definition of stratified random sampling.

39. CORRECT ANSWER: D
If n = original sample size, the variance of the sampling distribution of the mean =

σ^2/n. By increasing the size to 2n, the new variance = $\sigma^2/2n = \frac{1}{2}\sigma^2/n$.

40. CORRECT ANSWER: B
The population correction factor is often used if n > .05N, that is n is a significant part of N in terms of size.

———

EXAMINATION SECTION
TEST 1

DIRECTIONS: Each question or incomplete statement is followed by several suggested answers or completions. Select the one that BEST answers the question or completes the statement. *PRINT THE LETTER OF THE CORRECT ANSWER IN THE SPACE AT THE RIGHT.*

1. An unbiased coin is tossed 10 times and 7 heads appear. It is MOST likely that the number of heads appearing in the next ten tosses of the coin will be   1____

    A. 1   B. 2   C. 5   D. 6

2. The one of the following which is NOT a measure of the spread or variability of a distribution is the   2____

    A. range   B. mean deviation
    C. standard deviation   D. fiducial deviation

3. If $x_1 = X_1 - \overline{X}$ 3____
$x_2 = X_1 - \overline{X}$

    ....where $\overline{X} = \dfrac{\sum\limits_{i=1}^{N} X_1}{N}$, then $\sum\limits_{i=1}^{N} x_1 = \sum\limits_{i=1}^{N}(X_i - X) =$

$X_N = X_N - \overline{X}$

$\dfrac{\sum\limits_{i=1}^{N} X_i - N\overline{X}}{N}$.

Therefore, $\sum\limits_{i=1}^{N} x_i$ is equal to

    A. 0   B. $2N\overline{X}$ C. $\dfrac{2\sum\limits_{i=1}^{N} x_i}{N}$ D. $N\sum\limits_{i=1}^{N} x_i$

4. An urn contains 10 balls numbered from 1 to 10. The mean plus the variance of this population is MOST NEARLY   4____

    A. 20   B. 17   C. 14   D. 11

5. In a sample of 600 cases taken from a large population, the mean is 65 and the standard deviation is 5. The standard error of the mean is MOST NEARLY   5____

    A. .10   B. .20   C. .35   D. .40

6. If an unbiased coin is thrown 4 times, the probability of getting exactly 3 heads is   6____

    A. 1/16   B. 1/4   C. 5/16   D. 3/32

7. The correlation ratio, eta(n) is used in _____ correlation.   7____

   A. rank   B. serial
   C. regressive   D. non-linear

8. A study of the hourly earnings of workers in four firms showed the following: 8____

	Firm I	Firm II	Firm III	Firm IV
Mean hourly earnings Standard deviation of hourly earnings	$9.20	$10.20	$8,25	$11.10
	.46	.56	.55	.61

Using the coefficient of variation, the firm with the greatest internal wage differentials is Firm

   A. I   B. II   C. III   D. IV

9. If the size of a sample is tripled, the variance of the mean computed from the sample is multiplied by   9____

   A. $\sqrt{5}$ B. 4   C. 2/9   D. 1/3

10. A random sample of 100 cases shows that 50 percent of the persons in the sample have a certain characteristic.   10____
The 95 percent confidence interval for this percentage is MOST NEARLY from

   A. .35 to .61   B. .40 to .60
   C. .41 to .57   D. .43 to .59

11. Five units of each of four identically priced different brands of a certain electrical appliance were tested for length of service with the following results (in hundreds of hours):   11____

	Mean	Median	Mode	Range
Brand A	36.0	37.0	33.0	33-39
Brand B	35.6	38.0	38.0	30-38
Brand C	35.2	37.0	37.0	30-40
Brand D	34.8	35.0	39.0	30-39

Assume that the above results are similar to those which would be obtained from very large samples. If large quantities of this electrical appliance are to be purchased for a large housing development and minimum cost per hour of service is the selection criterion, it would be BEST to purchase Brand

   A. A   B. B   C. C   D. D

12. An urn contains 2 white and 3 black balls, while a second urn contains 4 white balls and 1 black ball.   12____
If an urn is selected at random and a single ball is drawn, the probability that it will be white is

   A. 7/10   B. 1/5   C. 5/8   D. 3/5

13. In cluster sampling, it is desirable that each cluster, within itself, should be   13____

   A. heterogeneous   B. homogeneous
   C. homoscedastic   D. normally distributed

14. When it is necessary to compare the variability of distributions described in different units, it is MOST desirable to use   14____

    A.   rank correlation   B.   analysis of variance
    C.   the coefficient of variation   D.   the normal distribution

15. The heights of all the men in the American Army were measured and found to be normally distributed with the mean equal to 68 inches and the standard deviation equal to 3 inches.   15____
The percentage of this population with heights from 65 inches to 74 inches is MOST NEARLY _____ percent.

    A. 82   B. 76   C. 75   D. 64

16. If an urn contains 95 white and 5 black balls, the probability that a random sample of 5 balls, drawn one at a time with replacement, will contain exactly one black ball is MOST NEARLY   16____

    A. .28   B. .20   C. .12   D. .04

17. A stationary time series is one which has no   17____

    A.   autocorrelation   B.   cyclical movement
    C.   correlative integration   D.   trend

18. Given the following data: 18____

$$\bar{x} = 3, \sigma \underline{x} = 2$$

$$\bar{y} = 3, \sigma y = 2 \qquad rxy = .6$$

The equation of the regression line of y on x is y =
    A.   .6x+1.2   B.   2x +3
    C.   .4x +.8   D.   5x +.3

19. The Doolittle method is used in   19____

    A.   testing hypotheses   B.   computing x^2
    C.   sequential sampling   D.   solving normal equations

20. Seven persons are tested on their knowledge of mathematics before and after taking a refresher course by being given Forri A of a certain test before the course begins and an equivalent Form B of this test after the course has ended. The scores are: 20____

	Score On	
Person	Form A	Form B
I	54	60
II	59	73
III	60	75
IV	62	80
V	66	90
VI	68	95
VII	72	91

The rank correlation coefficient of their scores on these two tests is
    A. .99   B. .96   C. .93   D. .90

21. If the value of a statistic approaches more and more closely the value of the population parameter as the sample size is indefinitely increased, the statistic is called

    A. consistent
    B. valid
    C. sufficient
    D. reliable

    21____

22. Ten persons are scored on two tests x and y with the following results:

Individual	1/4	2/4	3/2	4/1	5/0	6/-1	7/-2	8/-2	9/-3	10/-3
X										
y	4	2	1	3	-1	-2	-2	0	-2	-3

    The product-moment correlation between x and y is approximately
    A. .87   B. .79   C. .67   D. .54

    22____

23. The hypothesis that a sample whose mean value is x could have come from a population whose mean value is X and whose standard deviation is a may be tested by using

    A. Snedecor's F
    B. Goldbart's y
    C. Student's t
    D. Neyman's λ

    23____

24. The scores of a large group of high school seniors on three tests were correlated and the following correlation coefficients were obtained:
    General intelligence test and arithmetic ability $r = .7$
    General intelligence test and knowledge of $r = .5$
    English literature Arithmetic ability and knowledge of English literature $r = .4$
    The partial correlation coefficient between intelligence and arithmetic ability for this group, when knowledge of English literature is held constant, is MOST NEARLY

    A. .57   B. .60   C. .63   D. .66

    24____

25. In fitting a curve to the data on the population in a large city for each decade between 1790 and 1980, it would be MOST appropriate for a statistician to use a

    A. straight line
    B. parabola
    C. parameter
    D. logistic

    25____

26. Given the following data on unemployment in the United States:

Year (X)	Unemployment in Millions (Y)
1988 -3	10.4
1989 -2	9.5
1990 -1	8.1
1991 0	5.6
1992 1	2.7
1993 2	1.1
1994 3	0.7

    The equation of the least square trend line ($Y = a + bX$) is Y =
    A. 5.4-1.8X   B. 4.3-2.3X
    C. 6.7-3.5X   D. 6.2-2.9X

    26____

27. In using the chi-square technique for testing independence, if the data are tabulated in r rows and c columns, the number of degrees of freedom is equal to

    A. $\dfrac{r+c}{c-1}$ B. $(r-1)(c-1)$ C. $\dfrac{rc-1}{1-rc}$ D. $re + 1$

    27____

28. The U.S. Census Bureau uses the following seasonal index of unemployment: 28____

January	- 114.3	July	- 105.5
February	- 113.2	August	- 89.6
March	- 108.3	September	- 83.1
April	- 99.0	October	- 78.5
May	- 98.5	November	- 95.5
June	- 116.0	December	- 98.6

The Census Bureau reported that unemployment in December of one year was 4,100,000. Assuming that unemployment follows the seasonal pattern next year, it may be estimated that, in the high month, unemployment will be MOST NEARLY

A. 4,300,000   B. 4,500,000   C. 4,750,000   D. 4,800,000

29. Of the following statistical processes that one which does NOT involve an underlying assumption of the normality of population distribution is 29____

A. analysis of variance   B. produce-moment correlation
C. rank correlation   D. tetrachoric correlation

30. The use of moving averages will 30____

A. provide a mathematical expression for the curve
B. reveal the general trend more clearly
C. make possible predictions of values beyond the range of the original data
D. eliminate bias

31. The U.S. Bureau of Labor Statistics issues each month a Consumer Price Index which may be described as a(n) _____ type index. 31____

A. modified Laspeyres   B. Michele Ideal
C. moving average   D. adjusted Paasche

32. The daily rents of four families are listed in Stratum I as follows:
        Stratum I: $16, $28, $34, $36.
Similarly, the monthly rents of four other families are listed in Stratum II as follows:
        Stratum II: $42, $48, $58, $90.
If a simple random sample of size two is taken from Stratum I, and a simple random sample of size two is taken from Stratum II, the number of possible samples of size four that can be drawn is 32____

A. 15   B. 26   C. 36   D. 44

33. Use the data and sampling method given in Question 32. The variance of the rents in Stratum I is 81, and the variance of the rents in Stratum II is 457. The variance of the weighted sample mean X_s is given by the formula: 33____

$$V(\overline{X}_s) = W_1^2 (1 - \frac{n_1}{N_1}) \frac{\sqrt{1^2}}{n_1} + W_2^2 (1 - \frac{n_2}{N_2}) \frac{\sqrt{2^2}}{n_2} \text{ where}$$

W_i is the fraction of the population in Stratum i,

n_i is the size of the sample drawn from Stratum i,

N_i is the number of elements in Stratum i, and

$\sqrt{i^2}$ is the variance of the rents in Stratum i.

Using this formula on the above data, $V(\overline{X}_S)$ is approximately

A. 29   B. 34   C. 39   D. 44

34. Three of the four groups of forces which may be regarded as influencing an economic time series are seasonal variation, cyclical variation, and residual variation. The fourth is _____ variation.

    A. reticular   B. serial
    C. systematic   D. secular

34___

35. An index of industrial production is issued by the

    A. Bureau of Labor Statistics
    B. Bureau of the Census
    C. Federal Reserve Board
    D. Federal Trade Commission

35___

36. Orthogonal polynomials have been used by R.A. Fisher for

    A. time series analysis
    B. projection of experiments
    C. discriminant function analysis
    D. chi-square tests

36___

37. The following data show the correlations among three nornally distributed variables x, y, and z based on a large number of observations:

$$r_{xy} = .7, \ r_{xz} = .3, \ r_{yz} = -.1$$

The multiple correlation coefficient $R_{x.yz}$ is MOST NEARLY
    A. .71   B. .74   C. .78   D. .79

37___

38. Because of the extreme non-normality of the sampling distribution of r, the correlation coefficient, when testing the significance of an observed correlation coefficient, it is desirable to use

    A. Fisher's z   B. Hotelling's T^2
    C. Pearson's Type III   D. Poling's correction

38___

39. Data are available on the financial returns from each of a large sample of motion pictures which can be divided into two groups, those rated *above average* by movie critics, and those rated *below average*. A useful method, in this instance, for determining the correlation between excellence in dramatic art and financial success is _____ correlation.

    A. rank   B. peripatetic
    C. biserial   D. canonical

39___

40. A least squares line has been fitted to certain annual data and the following equation has been obtained:
               $Y = 10.6 + 0.7X$, (1973=0, and the X variable is in
               units of 1 year)
If the origin is shifted three years forward so that 1976 = 0, the resulting equation is $Y =$

    A. $29.5 + 0.6X$ B. $12.7 + 0.7X$
    C. $30.5 + 2.2X$ D. $12.7 + 1.7X$

40___

41. The Latin Square is used in   41____

    A. curve fitting   B. space series analysis
    C. experimental design   D. biserial correlation

42. Given the following data on the number of retirees in three city departments who chose   42____
    each of three possible options for receiving retirement allowances:

    | | Department | | | Row |
Option	I	II	III	Totals
A	30	25	44	99
B	39	30	30	99
C	30	44	25	99
Column Totals	99	99	99	

    Chi-square analysis can be used in determining whether there is a significant relation-
    ship between the department where the retiree worked and the option selected. The
    closeness of the relationship can be measured by computing the contingency coefficient,
    C, which for the data above is MOST NEARLY
    A. .10   B. .20   C. .30   D. .40

43. Sequential analysis is associated with the work of   43____

    A. R.A. Fisher   B. S.U. Wilks
    C. J.P. Neyman   D. A. Wald

44. In recent years, the mathematical problem of maximizing or minimizing a linear function   44____
    of many non-negative variables which, in addition, must satisfy certain linear restrictions,
    has received considerable attention.
    Such a problem has become known as a(n) _____ problem.

    A. linear programming   B. vertical hypothesis
    C. input-output   D. statistical decision

45. The MOST correct inference which can be drawn from Chebyshev's inequality is that the   45____
    proportion of an unknown distribution which lies within two standard deviations of the
    mean is MOST NEARLY _____ percent.

    A. 90   B. 88   C. 80   D. 75

46. Neyrian and Pearson have published important papers on   46____

    A. quantity control   B. testing hypotheses
    C. periodic correlation   D. time series analysis

47. In making certain studies of work experience over a period of years, the Bureau of Old   47____
    Age and Survivors Insurance has used a sample of persons whose Social Security
    account numbers end in certain selected digits.
    This type of sample is known as a _____ sample.

    A. systematic   B. residential
    C. purposive   D. cluster

48. The fraction of a finite population included in a sample affects the standard error of the mean computed from the sample as is apparent from the formula:

$$\bar{\sigma x} = \sqrt{\frac{N-n}{N-1}} \cdot \frac{\sigma}{\sqrt{n}}$$

where N is the number of members of the population and n is the number of members in the sample.

Thus, for a certain size sample, the percent by which the standard error of the mean, obtained from the formula under the assumption that the population is infinite, would be reduced if that same sample constituted 20 percent of a finite population is

   A. 25%   B. 18%   C. 12%   D. 10%

                                     48____

49. When sample sizes are small and assumptions of normality become untenable, or when the underlying distribution of the population is unknown, it is frequently possible to use methods of estimating parameters and testing hypotheses which are known as _____ methods.

   A. nonputative   B. nonparametic
   C. noniterative   D. nonlinear

                                     49____

50. The error committed in accepting a false null hypothesis is called a _____ error.

   A. Chi-square   B. Grumann
   C. Type II   D. Pearson Type III

                                     50____

51. When the statistician does not fix the sample size in advance, but proceeds to take one observation at a time until a decision can be made, subject to the desired risks of error, he is using a procedure called _____ sampling.

   A. conservative   B. sequential
   C. purposive   D. precision

                                     51____

52. A sample statistic which summarizes all of the relevant information which the observations contain concerning the population parameter is called a(n) _____ statistic.

   A. consistent   B. resistant
   C. efficient   D. sufficient

                                     52____

53. Suppose that drawings are made from an urn containing black and white balls in a known proportion, and that each ball drawn is returned to the urn, but only after the next drawing has been made. The probability that the (n+1) st ball drawn will be white is known if we know the color of the nth ball drawn and this probability is independent of what happened at the (n-1) st or earlier drawing.
Such trials are said to constitute a

   A. spurious sample   B. systematic sample
   C. Markov chain   D. Bernoullian series

                                     53____

54. In statistical quality control theory, the possibility that a batch of goods of acceptable quality will be rejected by the sampling scheme as a result of a pessimistic-looking sample is called the

   A. Producer's Risk   B. Consumer's Risk
   C. Corrective Function   D. Error Function

                                   54____

55. If T is distributed between -1/2 and +1/2 in a rectangular distribution, the cube root $Z = T^{1/3}$ is distributed in a_____ distribution.

    55____

    A. Vichy
    C. Type l
    B. u-shaped
    D. rectangular

56____

56. If $\sigma(\overline{X}_j)$ is defined as the probability that a variable X takes a particular value X_j, and

    G(T), the generating function, is defined as $G(T) = \frac{\Sigma}{j} \sigma(X_j)T^{X}J$, then the j generating

    function for an asymmetrical coin for which the probability of heads (Value = 1) is p, and of tails (Value = 0) is q, is

    A. 1/3 (T+1)
    C. 1/4 (pT+q)
    B. pT+q
    D. 1/5(1-T)

57. In order to test the hypothesis that a coin is not biased, it is decided to toss it five times and to reject the hypothesis if either five heads or five tails occur. If p, the true probability of getting a head in one toss, is acttally 1/2, the probability of rejecting the hypothesis can be calculated. Similarly, if p is really 2/3 or any other value, the probability of rejecting the hypothesis can be computed.
    The probability of rejecting the hypothesis of no bias, considered as a function of p, is called the

    57____

    A. error of Type III
    B. power series of Type II
    C. power function of the test
    D. axillary limit of the function

58. An axiomatic foundation for the theory of probability has been published by

    58____

    A. Siegall
    C. Pushkin
    B. Pearson
    D. Kolmogorov

59. Given an urn with four balls in it, either white or black, let Hu be the hypothesis that there are two white balls in the urn. The following experiment is designed to test whether Hu is to be accepted as the true hypothesis:

    59____

    A ball is drawn from the urn and its color is noted as 0 if it is white and 1 if it is black. This first ball is replaced in the urn and a second ball is drawn and the color noted.

    Assuming that Hu is true, the possible results are (0,0) or two white balls; (0,1) a white ball and then a black ball; (.1,0) a black ball and then a white ball; and (1,1) or two black balls; and each of these four possible results has a probability equal to 1/4. We may select any one of these four sample results as a CRITICAL REGION of size 1/4 and decide to reject Hu if the experiment produces this particular result. Otherwise, we do not reject Hu.
    If actually there is only one white ball in the urn, i.e., Hu is not true, the critical region which is best, in the sense that it gives us the greatest probability of correctly rejecting Hu, is

    A. (0,0)
    B. (0,1)
    C. (1,0)
    D. (1,1)

60. Four high jumpers tie for first place in a track meet. Since there are three medals, the four draw by lot for the gold medal. Then the three losers draw for the silver medal. Then the two remaining draw for the bronze medal. Jones, one of the four, reasons that he has one chance in four of getting the gold medal, plus one chance in three of getting the silver medal, plus one chance in two of getting the bronze medal and, therefore, he is certain that he will get a medal.

The one of the following which is an accurate statement of the probabilities associated with the distribution of the medals is that Jones has one chance in

    A.   three of getting the bronze medal
    B.   four of getting the gold medal
    C.   four of getting the silver medal
    D.   two of not getting a medal

60____

KEY (CORRECT ANSWERS)

1.	C	16.	B	31.	A	46.	B
2.	D	17.	D	32.	C	47.	A
3.	A	18.	A	33.	B	48.	D
4.	C	19.	D	34.	D	49.	B
5.	B	20.	B	35.	C	50.	C
6.	B	21.	A	36.	A	51.	B
7.	D	22.	A	37.	D	52.	D
8.	C	23.	C	38.	A	53.	C
9.	D	24.	C	39.	C	54.	A
10.	B	25.	D	40.	B	55.	D
11.	A	26.	A	41.	C	56.	B
12.	D	27.	B	42.	B	57.	C
13.	A	28.	D	43.	D	58.	D
14.	C	29.	C	44.	A	59.	D
15.	A	30.	B	45.	D	60.	C

SOLUTIONS TO PROBLEMS

1. CORRECT ANSWER: C

    Previous tosses of a coin are not relevant. Regardless of the number of heads which <u>had already</u> appeared, the most likely number of heads for the next 10 tosses is 5. Probability of heads on each toss = 1/2.

2. CORRECT ANSWER: D

    Fiducial means *based on trust,* which is not a mathematical measurement.

3. CORRECT ANSWER: A

    $$\sum_{i=1}^{n} x_i = x_1 + x_2 + x_3 + \dots + x_n$$

    $$= \sum_{i=1}^{n} x_i - N\bar{X} = \sum_{i=1}^{n} x_i - (N)\left(\frac{\sum_{i}^{n} x_i}{N}\right)$$

    $$= \sum_{i=1}^{n} x_i - \sum_{i=1}^{n} x_i = 0$$

4. CORRECT ANSWER: C

    Mean = (1+2+3+...+10)/10 = 55/10 = 5.5
    Variance = $\sum(x_i-\bar{x})^2/10$ =(1-5.5)^2/10 + (2-5.5)^2/10 +...(10-5.5)^2/10 = 8.25
    Mean + Variance = 5.5 + 8.25 = 13.75 ≈ 14

5. CORRECT ANSWER: B

    Standard error of the mean = standard deviation divided by the square root of the number of cases = $5/\sqrt{600}$ ≈ .20

6. CORRECT ANSWER: B

    $$\text{Probability of 3 heads} = (_4C_3)(\tfrac{1}{2})^3(\tfrac{1}{2})$$
    $$= (\frac{4 \cdot 3 \cdot 2}{1 \cdot 2 \cdot 3})(.125)(.5) = 1/4$$

7. CORRECT ANSWER: D

    Correlation ratio (n) measures a quantitative dependent factor against a qualitative independent factor.

8. CORRECT ANSWER: C

    The coefficient of variation = standard deviation divided by the mean. For Form III, this value = .55/8.25 = $.0\overline{6}$. This value is higher than the figures for Firms I, II, and IV.

9. CORRECT ANSWER: D

The variance of the mean $\sigma_{\overline{x}}^2 = \sigma^2/n$, when n = size of sample.

If the new sample size is $\sigma_{\overline{x}}^2$ becomes $\sigma^2/(3n)$.

10. CORRECT ANSWER: B

The 95% confidence interval is given by $.50 \pm 1.96 \dfrac{\sqrt{(.50)(.50)}}{100}$

$= .50 \pm .098 = .402$ to $.598$ or approx. .40 to .60.

11. CORRECT ANSWER: A

The best brand would have the highest mean and a range consisting of a relatively high low point and high point. Brand A seems to fit best.

12. CORRECT ANSWER: D

Probability of white ball = (Prob. of white) x (Prob of urn 1) + (Prob of white) x (Prob of urn 2) = (2/5)(1/2) + (4/5X1/2) = 3/5

13. CORRECT ANSWER: A

Each cluster should be a mixed representation of the original population.

14. CORRECT ANSWER: C

The coefficient of variation equals the standard deviation divided by the mean, expressed as a percent. Thus, it is not associated with specific units.

15. CORRECT ANSWER: A

The standard score for 65 is $(65-68) \div 3 = -1$ and the standard score for 74 is $(74-68) \div 3 = 2$. Using the Standard Normal Distribution table, the percent of data lying between -1 and 2 = 34.13% + 47.72% $\approx$ 82%.

16. CORRECT ANSWER: B

The probability that exactly one drawn ball is black = $(5)(.05)(.95)^4 \approx .20$

17. CORRECT ANSWER: D

A trend is a pattern which shows growth or a decrease over time, which stationary series don't have.

18. CORRECT ANSWER: A

The equation of the regression line is y = mx+b, where m = $(r_{xy})(5y)/5_x$ and b = $\overline{y} - m\overline{x}$. Use 5y in place of σ_y; 5x in place of σ_x. Then, m = (.6)(2)/2 = .6 and b = 3 - (.6)(3) = 1.2

19. CORRECT ANSWER: D

The Doolittle Method basically solves 2 linear equations in 2 variables by multiplying and adding to eliminate 1 variable.

20. CORRECT ANSWER: B

The rank correlation coefficient $r_s = 1 - \dfrac{6\Sigma d^2}{n(n^2-1)}$ where d = difference between ranks within each pair of data, and n = number of pairs. The ranks for persons I through VII on Form A are 1, 2, 3, 4, 5, 6, 7. On Form B, they are 1, 2, 3, 4, 5, 7, 6. Σd^2 =0+0+0+0+0+1+1=2

$$r_s = 1 - \frac{(6)(2)}{(7)(48)} \approx .96$$

21. CORRECT ANSWER: A

A statistic is consistent if, as the sample size is increased, the statistic approaches the parameter (of the population).

22. CORRECT ANSWER: A

The product-moment correlation between x and y,

$$r = \frac{\Sigma(x-\bar{x})(y-\bar{y})^2}{(n-1)(s_x)(sy)}.$$ For this example, $\bar{x} = \bar{y} = 0$, n = 10,

$$s_x = \frac{\sqrt{\Sigma(x-\bar{x})^2}}{n-1} \approx 2.67 \text{ and } sy = \frac{\sqrt{\Sigma(y-\bar{y})^2}}{n-1} \approx 2.4$$

So, $r = 50/[(19)(2.67)(2.4)] \approx .87$

23. CORRECT ANSWER: C

This distribution is used on small samples to test if the sample whose mean = m could have come from a population with mean x. A small sample has size less than 30.

24. CORRECT ANSWER: C

Let X_1 = Intelligence, X_2 = Arithmetic, X_3 = English Literature.

The partial correlation coefficient, $r_{12\cdot3} = (r_{12} - r_{13} r_{23})/\sqrt{(1-r_{13}^2)(1-r_{23}^2)}$

$= [.7 - (.5)(.4)]/\sqrt{(1-.5^2)(1-.4^2)} \approx .63$

25. CORRECT ANSWER: D

The logistic equation used is $y = S/[1+Ce^{-skt}]$, where y = population, S = maximum possible population, C = (S-yo)/yo with yo being initial population, t = time for population y, and k = constant.

26. CORRECT ANSWER: A

We solve $\Sigma Y = na + b\Sigma x$ and $\Sigma xy = a\Sigma x + b\Sigma x^2$. Since $n = 7$, we get $38.1 = 7a + 0b$ and $-51.3 = 0a + 28b$. Solving, $a = 5.4$ and $b = -1.8$.

27. **CORRECT ANSWER: B**

Using X^2 (chi-square) for independence, the number of degrees of freedom $= (r-1)(c-1)$.

28. **CORRECT ANSWER: D**

Since unemployment is highest in June, its values $= (116.0/98.6)(4,100,000) \approx 4,800,000$.

29. **CORRECT ANSWER: C**

This is called the Spearman rank correlation test, and it is a non-parametric method designed to measure the degree of association between two sets of ranked data. The population from which the data is extracted need not be normal.

30. **CORRECT ANSWER: B**

Moving averages tend to *smoothen* the data. With time series, the effects of seasonality and irregularity will be reduced. Thus, a general trend can be more easily viewed.

31. **CORRECT ANSWER: A**

As with the Consumer Price Index, the modified Lespeyres Price Index uses the base year as the denominator of the formula,

which is $\dfrac{\sum\limits_{i=1}^{n} P_{ti}Q_{ot}}{\sum\limits_{i=1}^{n} P_{oi}Q_{oi}} \times 100$, where P_{ti} = price in year t, P_{oi} = price in base year, and Q_{oi} = quantity in base year.

32. **CORRECT ANSWER: C**

The number of samples of size four $= (_4C_2)(_4C_2) = 6^2 = 36$

33. **CORRECT ANSWER: B**

$$V(\bar{x}_s) = (\frac{1}{2})^2(1-\frac{1}{2})(\frac{81}{2}) + (\frac{1}{2})^2(1-\frac{1}{2})(\frac{457}{2})$$
$$= 5.0625 + 28.5625 \approx 34$$

34. **CORRECT ANSWER: D**

This type of variation is also called a trend. This refers to a smooth upward or downward movement over a long (at least 15 years) time.

35. **CORRECT ANSWER: C**

This index will measure changes in the physical amount of output of manufacturing, mining, and utilities.

36. **CORRECT ANSWER: A**

Orthogonal polynomials are a computational method in determining curves to fit trend data in time series problems.

37. CORRECT ANSWER: D

$$R^2_{x.yz} = \frac{.7^2 + .3 - (2)(.7)(.3)(-.1)}{1 - (-.1)^2} = .6\overline{28}, \text{ so } R_{x.yz} \approx .79$$

38. CORRECT ANSWER: A

This is a transformation for an observed correlation coefficient, r, to a quantity, h, defined as

$$h = \frac{1}{2}|Log_e \left(\frac{1+r}{1-r}\right)| \text{ and also } s^2_h = \frac{1}{n-3}, n = \text{ number of pairs of data.}$$

39. CORRECT ANSWER: C

In this type of correlation, values which are similar seem to follow earlier values, especially true in trends related to time series.

40. CORRECT ANSWER: B

Since the new line will be parallel to the original line, the slope (.7) must be the same. The initial y value for the new line will be 10.6 + (.7)(3) = 12.7.

41. CORRECT ANSWER: C

This type of arrangement (Latin Square) permits each treatment to be applied exactly once under each level of the blocking variables.

42. CORRECT ANSWER: B

Each expected cell entry would be (99)(99)/297 = 33. The

contingency coefficient, C, is first computed with $\sum\limits_{i=1}^{9} (O_i - E_i.)^{2/E_i}$

= [36 + 128 + 242 + 36] ÷ 33 ≈ 13.4

Then, C = $\sqrt{13.4/(13.4+297)}$ ≈ .2078 ≈ .20

43. CORRECT ANSWER: D

Abraham Wald suggested the use of the maximum criterion in sequential analysis. This involves maximizing a payoff under pessimistic assumptions.

44. CORRECT ANSWER: A

This branch of mathematics involves linear inequalities identified by certain restrictions on the variables. The objective is then to either minimize or maximize a function of the variables.

45. CORRECT ANSWER: D

By Chebyshev's Theorem, at least $(1-1/k^2) \times 100$ percent of the given data must lie within k standard deviations of the mean. When $k = 2$, $(1-1/2^2) \times 100 = 75\%$

46. CORRECT ANSWER: B

In particular, the Neyman-Pearson Theorem is used to find the best critical region in conjunction with a likelihood ratio test.

47. CORRECT ANSWER: A

A particular restriction is being applied in order to reduce the actual population from which the sample will be drawn randomly.

48. CORRECT ANSWER: D

Let n be replaced by .20N. Then, $\dfrac{\sqrt{N-n}}{N-1} = \dfrac{\sqrt{.80N}}{N-1} \approx .894$. The percent reduction is

$(1-.894) \times 100 \approx 10\%$

49. CORRECT ANSWER: B

These tests are also called distribution-free, since they do not assume a normally distributed population.

50. CORRECT ANSWER: C

This error is committed when a false null hypothesis is accepted. Type I error means rejecting a true null hypothesis.

51. CORRECT ANSWER: B

In sequential sampling, each observation is taken in sequence until a sound decision can be made.

52. CORRECT ANSWER: D

A sufficient statistic utilizes all the relevant information which a sample contains about the parameter to be estimated in the population.

53. CORRECT ANSWER: C

With respect to a discrete random variable (color of each ball), a Markov chain explains future values based on a present event and only dependent on an immediately preceding event.

54. CORRECT ANSWER: A

This probability is also called a Type I error. It represents the probability that a batch of goods which meets the acceptable quality level will actually be rejected, based on sampling.

55. CORRECT ANSWER: D

$$f(T) = \frac{1}{\frac{1}{2}-(-\frac{1}{2})} = 1 \qquad\qquad f(z) = f(T^{1/3}) = 1$$

The ordinate must be 1 because the area under a probability distribution is $1 \cdot \sqrt[3]{1} = 1$. The probability distribution is unchanged.

56. **CORRECT ANSWER: B**

$$6(T) = \phi(0)T^\circ + \phi(1)T^1 = (q)(1) + (p)(T)$$
$$= pT + q$$

57. **CORRECT ANSWER: C**

The power function equals 1-3, where g is the probability of a Type II error.

58. **CORRECT ANSWER: D**

He constructed the foundation in set theory which was directly applied to probability in 1933.

59. **CORRECT ANSWER: D**

This represents the event of drawing 2 black balls, with replacement, one at a time.
If there is only 1 white ball, this probability is $(3/4)^2 = 9/16$.
The probabilities associated with (0,0), (0,1), and (1,0) are 1/16, 3/16, and 3/16, respectively. Thus, (1,1) has the highest probability.

60. **CORRECT ANSWER: C**

The probability that Jones will get a silver medal is equivalent to the probability of <u>not</u> getting the gold medal, then getting the silver medal.
Mathematically, this means $(3/4)(1/3) = 1/4$

117

BASIC FUNDAMENTALS OF STATISTICS

TABLE OF CONTENTS

Page

Basic Fundamentals of Statistics

I. SCORES: THEIR MEANINGS AND FORMS

"Whatever exists, exists in some amount."

As soon as measurements of any sort advance beyond the primitive statement that one thing is greater than, equal to, or less than another thing, we find the attempt to state results in numerical terms.

The meaning of such numerical statements should be clearly understood.

    A.   Discrete and Continuous Scores

There are certain kinds of measurement that result in scores that are *discrete* in the sense that there exist real gaps between the possible measurements that one can obtain. Thus the number of children in a family, or bills in a purse, increases only by whole numbers; one cannot find 5 1/2 children, or 7 1/4 bills, unless one practices mutilation. Other measures give *continuous* scores in the sense that the scores are theoretically capable of any degree of subdivision. Scores on tests are usually given in units, as 68 or 75; but with more accurate tests, scores of 77.4 or 86.273 would also be possible. Nearly all measurements in psychology and education deal with continuous series of scores rather than with discrete series, and the following discussion deals throughout with the statistical treatment of continuous series. Some modification of the formulas used with continuous series is necessary before one can apply them to discrete series.

    B.   Raw and Derived Scores

The score actually obtained in making a measurement is called a *raw score.* If a pupil makes a score of 59 on a test, that is his raw score. Raw scores do not by themselves indicate if they are high or low; a score of 59 might be high on one test and low on another. If a pupil made a score of 59 on an intelligence test, that might be translated to mean that he achieved a mental age of 12 years, an IQ of 108, a percentile rank of 78, etc. All these interpretative measures would be called *derived scores,* as they are derived from the raw score. A derived score tells us much more about the quality of a performance than the raw score does. Many kinds of derived scores will be described below.

II. THE ARRANGEMENT

Suppose that a certain class takes a test and makes the following scores: 92, 88, 97, 95, 100, 58, 90, 94, 72, 91, 83, 88, 83, 87, 82, 78, 64, 69, 97, 95, 86, 85, 85, 89, 77, 61, 74, 59. Until we arrange them in some different way we cannot tell much about these scores. (Note: most of the computations in the Appendix are based on this series of scores.)

    A.   Rank Order

With a small number of scores, it is often profitable to arrange them in rank order, with the highest at one end and the lowest at the other. From the rank order one can very easily determine the highest score, the lowest score, the midscore and percentile scores. One method of correlation is based on the rank order. Confusion will be avoided if the lowest score is always given rank one. The only difficulty that arises in constructing a rank order is in regard to tie scores. In such a case, the ranks covered by the tied scores are averaged, and that average rank is given to each. Example: If two scores are tied for second rank, they cover ranks two and three; $\frac{2+3}{5} = 2.5$, and than rank is given to each. The next following score is given rank four. If the ranking is done properly, the last score should come out with a rank equal to the number of scores, except where there is a tie for last place.

B. Tabulation

Tabulation consists essentially in dividing the scores into groups, all groups covering equal portions of the total range of scores, and arranging the groups in rank order. When the groups, which are called *classes,* are arranged in a vertical column, and the number of scores falling in each class is indicated by a number, the tabulation is called a *frequency distribution. A* frequency distribution gives us a fairly clear picture of the way the scores are distributed. It is necessary to get the frequency distribution before one can represent the results graphically, or use any of the shortcut methods of computation. It usually takes less time to tabulate scores than it does to rank them, unless the number of scores is very small.

Before tabulating, it is necessary to choose the size of the class interval to be used. To do this, first subtract the lowest from the highest score, getting the range. Choose as the size of the interval a number that will divide the range into not less than 10 or more than 20 classes. Arrange the classes in a vertical column, with the highest at the top. In table 1, Appendix, a class interval of 5 has been used. Note that the lowest class, 55-59.99, means anything from 55.0 up to but not including 60; and that its midpoint is 57.5, not 57.0. Often the class is written simply as 55-59; in that case, it really means 55.0-59.99. For each score in the series, place a tally (/) to the right of the class in which the score belongs. The frequency column simply states in numbers the number of tallies, or scores, in each class.

C. Graphical Representation

A graph, or pictorial representation, often tells a story much more vividly than a table. There are two main kinds of graphs for representing score distributions, the histogram and the frequency polygon. In both, the classes are represented by equal distances along a horizontal line, with the lowest at the left. The difference is that in the histogram a horizontal line is drawn above the class to indicate the number of scores, and these lines are connected by vertical lines; while in the frequency polygon the number of scores is represented by a dot above the midpoint of the class, and the dots are joined by straight lines. Note that the histogram represents each score by a similar unit of area; the frequency polygon does not. The frequency polygon is generally used when two or more distributions are to be compared graphically, as similarities and differences in shape stand out more clearly, due to the oblique lines, than they do with histograms. The Appendix contains a histogram and a frequency polygon for the same set of scores.

III. MEASURES OF CENTRAL TENDENCY, OR AVERAGES

There are several kinds of averages, or measures of central tendency, of which only three -- the median, the mean, and the mode -- are used to any extent in psychological and educational measurement. All averages represent the whole distribution of scores by a single number. It must be remembered that most score distributions contain some scores that are far from the average. Nevertheless, the average is the most useful single statistical measure that one can find out about a group of scores.

A. The Median (Mdn.)

The median is that value such that half of the scores are greater than or equal to it, and half of the scores are less than or equal to it. If the scores are arranged in rank order, the median is the middle score, or mid-score, and can be obtained by counting from either end of the rank order. Note that the extreme scores can be either close to or far from the median without affecting its computation.

The median is preferable to the mean when quick computation is desired; when extreme or inaccurate scores should not influence the average; and when percentile scores are to be obtained. The norms (see below for the meaning of this term) of many intelligence and educational tests are stated in terms of median and percentile scores, and when using such tests the median is to be preferred to the mean.

B.   The Mean (M)

The mean is the measure popularly called "the average" and can be simply obtained by adding together all of the scores and dividing by the number

$$M = \frac{\Sigma m}{N}$$ In the Formula means "sum of," m refers to an individual score, and N

means the number of scores. The exact size of each score counts in finding the mean, while only the scores near the middle of the distribution are important in determining the median. The mean should be used when a standard deviation or coefficient of correlation is to be found, and when every score should count in the average. It involves somewhat more arithmetical computation than the median.

Unless the number of cases is small, time can be saved by computing the mean from scores grouped in a frequency distribution, rather than from ungrouped scores. Multiply the midpoint of each class by the frequency in that class; i.e.,

$$M = \frac{F \text{ X Midpoint}}{N}$$. A still shorter method is available, in which one takes the mid-

point of some class as a guessed mean, and then calculates a correction which is added to the guessed mean. This is profitable when the number of scores is fairly large. For details of this "short method," consult a standard text.

C.   The Mode

The mode is simply the score that occurs the greatest number of times. There may be more than one mode in a score distribution. When the scores are grouped, the midpoint of the class that contains the greatest frequency is called the crude mode. The mode is greatly influenced by chance factors, and so is ordinarily of not much significance. It should be used when one wants the most frequent score, or when one wants a very rough average without calculation.

IV.   MEASURES OF THE DISTRIBUTION OF SCORES

A.   The Normal Curve

Scores in a great many human traits distribute themselves so as to form a symmetrical, bell-shaped frequency polygon, which is called a normal curve, normal distribution curve, normal probability curve, etc. Normal curves are obtained when the results are influenced by a large number of factors, each acting separately in an apparently chance way. For instance, if one tosses 20 pennies 1000 times, and plots the number of times each possible combination of heads and tails comes out, the results will form a normal curve. The normal curve is very important statistically, because all normal curves have similar statistical properties. Knowing the mean and standard deviation of a normal curve, one can deduce all of the other characteristics of the distribution. In a perfectly normal curve the mean, median, and mode all fall on the same score. Very often distributions are obtained which closely approximate normal distributions, but are not exactly normal; if the difference is slight, they may be treated as normal curves. When a distribution is lop-sided, with the scores piled up more on one side of the mean than on the other, it is said to be skewed. A large departure from the true normal curve may be due to a small number of cases, or may indicate that the trait is distributed in a way that is not fundamentally normal.

B.   Importance of Measures of Distribution

Two groups may have the same average scores on a test, but be widely different. All the members of one class may make very similar scores, while the members of the other class may differ widely. For instance, 3, 6, 9, 12, and 15 have the same mean as 7, 8, 9, 10, and 11. This matter of the spread, scattering, variability, or distribution of scores is often very important. It can be roughly estimated from a graph, but for accuracy one of several available statistical measures should be used. These measures of distribution are really valid only for distributions that are fundamentally normal.

C. Measures of Distribution

1. The Range is simply the difference between the highest and lowest scores. It is the easiest measure of distribution to obtain, but the least dependable, because factors that have little effect on the distribution as a whole may have a marked effect on the on the extreme scores.

2. The Average Deviation (A.D.), sometimes called the mean deviation, is the mean of the deviations of the separate scores from the mean. The deviation of any score is the difference between that score and the mean. In getting the mean of the deviations, no attention is paid to plus and minus signs. Although relatively easy to obtain, the A.D. is less useful than the standard deviation, and. is being used less and less.

With grouped scores, the A.D. can be obtained by getting the deviation of each class midpoint from the mean. Each deviation is then multipled by the corresponding frequency. The mean of these deviations is then obtained, disregarding plus and minus signs. A "short method," in which deviations are taken from a guessed mean and a correction applied afterward, saves arithmetic because it eliminates multiplying by numbers containing decimals.

3. The Standard Deviation (S.D. or the Greek letter sigma (6). In calculating this measure, the deviation of each score from the mean is obtained, as with the A.D. Instead of simply averaging the deviations, however, each deviation is squared before averaging, and the square root of the average is extracted. This square root is the standard deviation -- it is the square root of the mean of the squared deviations.

$$\text{S.D.} = \sqrt{\frac{\Sigma D^2}{N}}$$

The S.D. has many uses. It has a constant relationship to the shape of the normal curve. Knowing the mean and the S.D. of a normal distribution, one can determine the percent of the total number of scores that lie between any two scores, by referring to a special table. Approximately 68% of the scores in any normal curve lie between the mean and the scores 1 S.D. above and below the mean; approximately 95% lie between the mean and the scores 2 S.D.'s above and below the mean; and over 99% of the scores are less than 3 S.D.'s above or below the mean (see the illustration of a normal curve in the Appendix). If we wanted to compare the variability of one set of scores with that of another, we simply compare their S.D.'s; the one with the larger S.D. has the greater spread of scores. The S.D. is the most valuable of the various measures of distribution, although its computation takes longer than that of the A.D. or Q. It must be computed if one wants to get T Scores or a product-moment coefficient of correlation (These are explained below).

As with the M and A.D., arithmetic can be lessened by computing

$$\text{S.D.} = \frac{\Sigma (F D^2)}{N}$$

the S.D. from grouped scores. See Table 2 in the Appendix for examples of the calculation of the A.D. and S.D. from grouped scores. There is also a "short method" of computing the S.D., in which deviations are taken from a guessed mean, and a correction applied.

4. The Probable Error (P.E.). The P.E. is obtained by multiplying the S.D. by .6745. In a normal distribution exactly 50% of the cases lie between the mean and the scores one P.E. above or below the mean; the other 50% of the scores are more than one P.E. away from the mean. Practically all cases in a normal distribution are less than 4 P.E.'s away from the mean.

5. The Quartile Deviation (Q). One often wants to locate the middle 50% of a group of scores. The first quartile point, Q_1, is that score below or equal to which are 25%

of the scores in the distribution. The third quartile point, Q_3, is that score below or equal to which 75% of

the scores lie. The middle 50% of the scores can be found by subtracting Q_1 from Q_3

$$Q = \frac{Q_3 - Q_1}{2}$$

The quartile deviation is half of the range of scores. It is one-half of the range covered by the middle 50% of the scores. In a perfectly normal distribution Q and P.E. are identical. It is customary to use Q as the measure of variability when the median is used as the measure of central tendency.

V. DERIVED SCORES

If one is told that a person has made a score of 43 on a test, that in itself means very little, as the meaning of a score depends on many factors. The test itself may have a total possible score of 50, 100, or 150. The mean may be below 30 or above 70. The scores may be grouped closely together or spread over a wide range. For this reason a raw score must be interpreted in some way before it tells much about the goodness of the performance.

A. Percent Scores

Teachers often express scores in terms of the percent of the total possible score. An easy way to do this is to score the test so as to have a total possible score of 100. This is fairly satisfactory, but has some shortcomings. One teacher may give harder tests than another, or score of 85%. This sometimes happens when the students in the two classes have equal knowledge; sometimes the better class may get the lower average.

B. Distance from the Average

If we know that a score is 5 points above or below the mean or median, we know more about it than if we simply know the raw score or percent score. However, 5 points may be a big difference on one test and a small difference on another test.

C. Percentile Scores

A percentile score states the percent of the total number of scores that are below or equal to a particular score. For instance, the statement that the raw score of 67 on a test stands at the 83rd percentile means that 83% of the scores in the distribution are at or below 67. The median is the 50th percentile; Q_1 is the 25th percentile; Q_3 is the 75th percentile. The percentile score tells us not merely whether a score is above or below the median, but gives us also its exact place in the rank order. Because percentile scores are easy to compute and help greatly in the interpretation of scores, most psychological and educational tests designed for general use are accompanied by tables giving the percentile values of all of the possible raw scores on the test.

These values are based on results previously obtained with the test. Often separate percentile tables are given for each age or grade, so that one can determine just how each pupil in a group stands in comparison with the much larger group used in determining the tables.

Since in a normal distribution the scores are much more frequent near the median than they are near the extremes, percentile scores are not directly proportional in size to raw scores. For instance, there is more of a difference between the raw scores of two pupils with percentile ranks of 90 and 95 than there is between the ra.w scores of two pupils with percentile ranks of 50 and 55. For this reason one cannot combine a pupil's scores on different tests by averaging his percentile scores. The best way to average scores on different tests, with different averages and different variabilities, is to use T Scores, which are explained below.

To find the raw scores corresponding to any percentile value, first multiply N by the percentile value, and then count up that many scores from the bottom of the rank order, or down from the top. The median is the 50th percentile; to locate it, count 50% of the scores from either end of the rank order. The 60th percentile, in a group of 25 scores, is the 15th from the lowest. When the desired score is fractional, and when the percentile score is calculated from grouped scores, interpolation is necessary. In Table 1, Appendix, illustrations are given of the calculation of the Median, 25th percentile, 75th percentile, and Q. The calculation of the median may be explained as follows: 50% of N is 14. There are 12 scores below the 85 - 89.99 class, and 7 scores in that class; therefore the median is 2/7ths of the way up in that class. Since the class covers 5 scores, multiply 2/7ths by 5; add this to 85.0, the lower limit of the class, and the result is the median. Other percentiles are calculated in the same way.

D.   T Scores

Since the S.D. has a constant relation to the shape of the normal curve, a score which is a certain distance above the mean on one test has the same relative value as a score which is the same distance above the mean on another test, if the distances are divided by the S.D. in each case, and equated on that basis. In other words, a score which is two S.D.'s above the mean on one test is equivalent to a score which is two S.D.'s above the mean on another test. T Scores are scores stated in terms of what fraction of an S.D. a score is above or below the mean. Because T Scores are always proportional to the raw scores, the T Scores of the same individual on different tests can be combined by simple averaging. This is the best way to combine scores from several different tests into a total score.

To translate raw scores into T Scores, first subtract the mean from each score, and divide each remainder by the S.D. This will be plus if the score is above the mean and minus if below the mean. Such scores are called "standard deviation scores." Multiply the standard deviation score by 10, and add 50; the result is a T Score. The possible range of T Scores is from 0 to 100, and the mean always has a T Score value of 50.

E.   Mental Age (M.A.)

Mental age is a kind of derived score used with intelligence tests. The M.A. corresponding to any raw score may be defined as the age of the group of children who on the average make that raw score. Example: A child makes a score of 43 on an intelligence test. 43 is the average raw score on this test of children 9 years, 3 months old. The child's M.A. is therefore 9 years, 3 months. A child's mental age increases as he gets older. Children of different chronological ages (C.A.'s) may have the same M.A.'s.

F.   Intelligence Quotient (I.Q.)

The I.Q. is the M.A. divided by the C.A. A child who is above average mentally always has an I.Q. above 100, and a child below average has an I.Q. below 100. The I.Q. remains roughly constant as a child grows older; it is an indication of the rate of mental growth, or brightness.

G. Educational Age (E.A.)

This is similar to the M.A., except that it applies only to tests of educational achievement or knowledge. A child has an E.A. of 10 years when he makes a score on an educational test equal to the average score of 10 year old children.

H. Educational Quotient (E.Q.)

This is the E.A. divided by the C.A. It indicates the rate of educational progress, while the E.A. indicates the present educational attainment. The E.A. and E.Q. are obtained from standardized tests covering several subjects. Ages and quotients can also be obtained for individual subjects, as reading age, reading quotient, arithmetic age, etc.

I. Achievement Quotient (A.Q.)

This is an indication of how a child's educational achievement compares with his intelligence. It is obtained by dividing the E.A. by the M.A., or by dividing the E.Q. by the I.Q. A child with an E.A. of 8 years an an M.A. of 10 years has an A.Q. of 80; a child with an E.Q. of 120 and an I.Q. of 100 has an A.Q. of 120.

J. Norms

Norms are groups of scores for a particular test which have been obtained from large groups of subjects, and which are used for interpreting new results obtained with the test. Percentile scores, T Scores, mental and educational ages and quotients are all different ways of stating the norms. Usually the author of an intelligence or achievement test states his norms in more than one of these ways. Another kind of norm sometimes used is the *grade norm,* where the average score given is for a grade rather than for a chronological age.

VI. COMPARISONS OF GROUPS

One often wants to compare the results of two groups on the same test. A simple statement of the means or medians of the two groups is not sufficient, because there may be much or little overlapping between the two groups (see examples at the right.) A commonly used device is to state the percent of one group that exceeds the median of the other  group. If this is close to 50%, the amount of overlapping is great; if close to 0 or 100, the overlapping is relatively slight.

A problem that occurs frequently in psychological and educational measurement is the question whether a difference that has been found between two measures is reliable; in other words, would a similar difference be found again and again if the measurements were repeated. This is determined by comparing the obtained difference with the standard error of the difference, or the probable error of the difference. The exact meaning of these two statistical measures need not be explained here. Differences are not considered to be completely reliable unless they are at least three times their standard error or four times the probable error. Example: The mean I.Q. of another class; the standard error of the difference is 1.3 points. Since the difference is less than 3 times its standard error, it is not reliable -- it may be due purely to chance, and a repetition may show no such difference.

VII. CORRELATION

One often wants to know whether there is any relation between two sets of results obtained from the same subjects. The most frequently used method of measuring such a relationship is to calculate a coefficient of correlation. This is a quantitative measure of the degree of relationship between two sets of measures for the same group of individuals. There are two widely used methods of measuring correlation. The simpler of these is the rank-difference method, devised by Spearman. This is based on the comparison of the rank orders in the two sets of measures, disregarding the actual size of the raw scores. It is much easier to calculate, and is usually used when the number of cases is small. It is somewhat less accurate than the product-moment method, devised by Pearson, which uses the raw scores. The symbol for the coefficient of correlation obtained by the rank-difference method is the Greek letter rho; for the product-moment coefficient, the letter r.

The student who wishes to learn how to compute r should refer to a basic reference. The computation of rho is relatively simple, and will be briefly outlined. The rank order for each set of measures is first obtained. For each subject the two ranks are placed side by side. The D or difference column records the difference between the two ranks, for each subject. These differences are then squared, and the squared differences are added up. This total is multipled by 6, and is the numerator of a fraction. The denominator of the fraction is $N(N^2-1)$. Rho is obtained by subtracting the fraction from 1.00. Consult Table 3 for an illustration.

A. Interpretation of the Coefficient of Correlation

Coefficients of correlation range in size from plus 1.00 to minus 1.00. Both of these values indicate a perfect relationship or correspondence. Plus 1.00 indicates that the person with the highest score on one trait also has the highest score on the other, the second highest is also second highest on the second, etc. Minus 1.00 means that the highest on one trait is the lowest on the other, the second highest on one is next to the lowest on the other, etc. An r of zero indicates that there is a complete absence of relationship between the two sets of measurements; those high on one trait may be either high or low on the other. Intermediate values (+.53,-.40, etc.) are not percents, an an r of approximately .80 indicates only half as close a relationship an an r of 1.00. Customarily an r of less than .40 is considered low, .40 - .70 substantial, and above .70, high. But even an r of .80 contains an occasional marked exception to the general relationship. Before we can predict a person's score on one trait with accuracy from a knowledge of his score on another trait, we should have an r above .90 between the two traits.

It should be noted that the presence of a correlation between two traits does not prove that one is the cause of the other; it merely indicates the presence of a relationship between the two. For instance, in an 8th grade class there is a minus correlation between height and I.Q. Neither of these traits is the cause of the other; the relationship is due to the fact that the younger children in the class are both smaller and brighter than the older children.

B. Uses of Correlation

One of the important uses of correlation is in *prediction*. *If* there is a high correlation between two traits, one can predict a person's score on one from a knowledge of his score on the other, with better than the chance success. A very high correlation, however, is necessary for accurate prediction.

C. Reliability

In using a test, it is important to know if the results obtained are close to what would be obtained if the measurements are repeated. By reliability we mean the extent to which the same test (or two equivalent forms of the same test) will give similar results when used on the same subjects more than once. Reliability is indicated by correlation. *Retest reliability* is the correlation between two sets of scores on the same test obtained from the same subjects. *Split-half reliability* is the correlation between scores on the two halves of a test; to make this comparable to retest reliability, a special formula (the Spearman-Brown Formula) is applied. A test to be really reliable, should have reliability over .90 as measured in both ways. Reliability is essentially the consistency with which a test will give the same results on repeated administration.

D. Validity

The validity of a test is its most important characteristic, and also the one hardest to measure. By validity we mean the degree of perfection to which a test measures what it is supposed to measure. Students often confuse validity with reliability. Remember that reliability measures the consistency of a test, the extent to which it will give the same results over and over again. A test may be reliable, without measuring what it is supposed to measure. For instance, one could measure the circumference of the skull very reliably, but the result would be an exceedingly poor indication of intelligence-- as a measure of intelligence this measure, although reliable, would be totally invalid. A history test consisting entirely of dates to be identified might give very reliable results, but they could be invalid as a measure of understanding the significance of historical events.

The usual way of measuring the validity of a test is to correlate the results with some criterion -- that is, with some other measure of the trait in question, which is already known to be valid. The big difficulty in establishing the validity of a new test is to find a satisfactory criterion. For instance, one should not look for an extremely high correlation with teacher's marks and estimates, because the test is expected to be a better measure than the teacher's marks are. Also, a perfect correlation with other tests that are known to be only partly valid is not desirable. Ordinarily a test is correlated with each of a few partly satisfactory criteria, and its validity is estimated from the results.

―――――――――

APPENDIX
Table 1 - Calculation of the Mean, Median, and Q

SCORES	MIDPOINT	TALLIES	F(FREQUENCY)	F x MIDPOINT
100-104.99	102.5	/	1	102.5
95- 99.99	97.5	////	4	390.0
90- 94.99	92.5	////	4	370.0
85- 89.99	87.5	++++ //	7	612.5
80- 84.99	82.5	///	3	247.5
75- 79.99	77.5	//	2	155.0
70- 74.99	72.5	/	2	145.0
65- 69.99	67.5	//	1	67.5
60- 64.99	62.5	//	2	125.0
55- 59.99	57.5		2	115.0
			N = 28	2330.0

HISTORGRAM

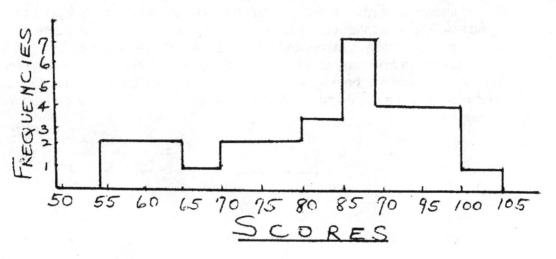

The Mean

$$M = \frac{(Fx\ Midpoint)}{N} = \frac{2330.0}{28} = 83.2$$

The Median

    50% of N = 14. There are 12 scores below the 85-89.99 interval, leaving 2 scores to go. There are 7 scores in that class, and the class covers 5 scores. 2/7 X 5 = 1.4.

    Median = 85.0 + 1.4 = 86.4

Frequency Polygon

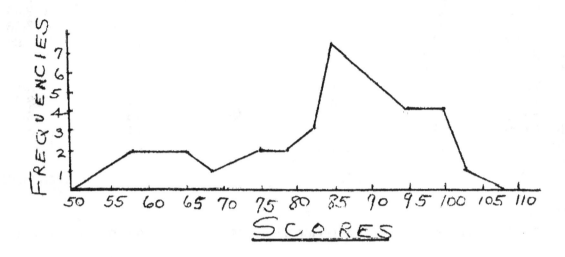

The Quartile Deviation

$$Q = \frac{Q_3 - Q_1}{2}$$

$$= \frac{92.5 - 75.0}{2}$$

$$= 8.75$$

$Q_3 =$ 75th percentile. 75% of 28 = 21. There are 19 scores below 90.0. 90.0 + 2/4 X 5 = 92.5

$Q_1 =$ 25th percentile. 25% of 28 = 7. 7 scores bring us exactly up to 75.0; therefore Q_1 = 75.0

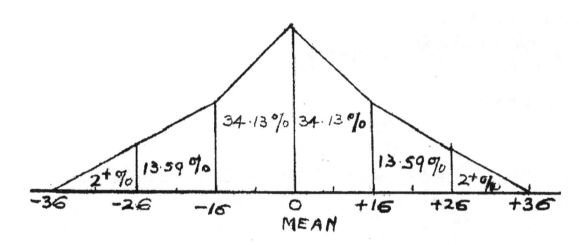

A THEORETICAL NORMAL CURVE

Table 2 - Calculation of the A. BY, S.D., and P.E.

SCORES	MIDPOINT	F	D(DEVTATION)	FD	FD²
100-104.99	102.5	1	19.3	19.3	372.49
95- 99.99	97.5	4	14.3	57.2	817.96
90- 94.99	92.5	4	9.3	37.2	345.96
85- 89.99	87.5	7	4.3	30.1	129.43
80- 84.99	82.5	3	- 0.7	- 2.1	1.47
75- 79.99	77.5	2	- 5.7	-11.4	64.98
70- 74.99	72.5	2	-10.7	-21.4	228.98
65- 69.99	67.5	1	-15.7	-15.7	246.49
60- 64.99	62.5	2	-20.7	-41.4	856.98
55- 59.99	57.5	2	-25.7	-51.4	1320.98
M= 83.2		N=28		257.2	4385.72

NOTES

1. For each class, the deviation is the difference between the mean and the midpoint of that class.
2. The FD^2 column is obtained by multiplying each FD by the corresponding D. It is $F \times D^2$, not $F^2 \times D^2$.
3. In adding up the FD column to get the A.D., the minus signs are disregarded. There are no minus signs in the FD^2

The Average Deviation

$$A.D. = \frac{\Sigma FD}{N} = \frac{287.2}{28} = 10.29$$

The Standard Deviation

$$S.D. = \sqrt{\frac{\Sigma(FD^2)}{N}} = \sqrt{\frac{4385.72}{28}} = \sqrt{56.63} = 12.52$$

The Probable Error

P.E. = .6745 X S.D. = .6745 X 12.52 = 8.44

Table 3 - Calculation of the Rank-Difference Coefficient of Correlation

Individual	Score on Test 1	Score on Test 2	Rank on Test 1	Rank on Test 2	D	D
A	18	20	7	4	3	9
B	24	17	4	7	3	9
C	22	19	5	5.5	0.5	0.25
D	27	21	1.5	3	1.5	2.25
E	26	25	3	2	1	1
F	27	26	1.5	1	0.5	0.256
G	20	19	6	5.5	0.5	0.25
N = 7					ΣD^2	=22.00

NOTES

1. Each entry in the "D" or difference column is the difference between the two ranks attained by that individual.
2. Note that, in getting the rank orders, two tied scores get the average of the two ranks covered; the following score gets the next rank.

$$\text{rho} = 1 - \frac{6\,\Sigma D^2}{N(N^2-1)} = 1 - \frac{6 \times 22.00}{7(49-1)} = 1 - \frac{132}{336} = +.61$$

BRIEF GLOSSARY OF STATISTICAL TERMS

BRIEF GLOSSARY OF STATISTICAL TERMS

I. DESCRIPTIVE STATISTICS (Descriptive statistics simply summarize in numerical terms the characteristics of a set of data. Such characteristics include measures of central tendency, spread, correlation, and the like.)

A. Frequency distribution

This is a tabulation, sometimes presented in graphical form, showing the frequencies of the value of the variable when these values are arranged in order of magnitude. The frequency distribution is typically the first step in analyzing a set of data.

B. Measures of the average or the central tendency

The three MOST common indices are the mean, the median, and the mode.

1. The mean is the arithmetic average, usually designated as M or X. It is computed by summing X all the scores and dividing by the number of measurements in the set.
2. The median is the middle value in a set of scores that is, the point on the scale of the frequency distribution below and above which exactly 50% of the observation occur.
3. The mode is the most common value in a frequency distribution. It is therefore possible for a distribution to have more than one mode.

Of the three measures listed above, the mean is the MOST commonly used, since it lends itself most readily to treatment by inferential statistics. The median has the advantage of being much easier to compute when the number of cases is 50 or less, and is also less influenced by extreme values. The mode is the MOST easily determined of the three, since it can usually be seen through directed inspection of the frequency distribution. The PRINCIPLE disadvantage of the mode is the difficulties it presents for inferential analysis.

C. Measures of variation

Summary description of the frequency distribution requires not only identification of the central tendency but some indication of the extent of spread of dispersion about this central value. Measures of the variation are used for this purpose.

1. The range is the simplest measure of dispersion. It is simply the difference between the smallest and largest measurement in the series. Like the mode, the range is readily determined, but does not lend itself to statistical treatment.
2. The standard deviation or Sigma (symbolized by SD or Z) is the MOST important, frequently used measure of dispersion. Algebraically, the standard deviation is obtained by expressing each measure as a deviation from the mean, squaring this deviation, summing all the squares, dividing by the number of observations, and taking the square root of this last value. In short, the standard deviation is the root mean square. The standard deviation may be used to compare the relative spread of two or more distributions. The standard deviation also serves as the basis for transforming distributions based on quite different units to the same scale. This is accomplished by expressing each measurement as a deviation from its mean and then dividing this deviation by

the standard deviation to yield what is called a standard score or z-score. For example, in standard tests of achievement, scores in different subject matters are made comparable by transforming them into standard scores.

3. The variance is the square of the standard deviation. It is seldom used as a measure of dispersion all by itself, but it is important as the basis for inferential statistics which have to take into account the amount of dispersion in the data (see analysis of variance below).

D. Measures of Correlation

Measures of correlation or association describe the extent to which one variable is related to another.

1. The MOST common measure of association is the Pearson Product-Moment Correlation Coefficient designated by r. Perfect correspondence between two variables is expressed by an r of 1.00; perfect inverse correspondence (i.e., as one increases the other decreases) is expressed by an r of 1.00; complete lack of correspondence is reflected by an r of 0.00. The correlation coefficient should not be interpreted as a per cent. For example, the fact that the correlation between height and weight is approximately .80 does not mean that one can predict height from weight correctly 80% of the time. Whether a correlation is to be regarded as high or low depends on the variables involved and the question being asked. For example, a correlation of .60 between an intelligence test administered in grade school and subsequent performance in college would be regarded as spectacularly high. The same correlation betwen two forms of an individual intelligence test such as the Stanford-Binet would be unacceptably low. The last example illustrates a common application of the correlation coefficient as an index of reliability; that is, the extent to which the same or presumably equivalent measurement procedures yield similar results.

2. The ranked correlation coefficient is a measure of association based on ranks rather than raw scores. It also ranges from -1.00 to +1.00. It is much easier to compute an r when the number of cases is relatively small, but it is not quite as reliable.

II. INFERENTIAL STATISTICS (Inferential statistics go one step further and measure the extent to which a descriptive statistic based on a particular sample may be regarded as an estimate of characteristics of the larger universe from which the sample is drawn. Examples of inferential statistics include all tests of statistical significance.)

A. The MOST common use of inferential statistics is to determine the extent to which a result based on a particular sample can be regarded as an accurate estimate of the state of affairs in the total universe from which the sample is drawn. In other words, inferential statistics are used to determine the extent to which an obtained result might vary from the true one as a function of chance. Such inferential statistics are called tests of statistical significance and are evaluated in terms of the probability level (P) that the obtained result could have occurred by chance. These levels of probability, also called confidence limits, are set arbitrarily usually at either the 1% or 5% level; that is, the level at which the obtained result would be obtained by chance either one or five times out of a hundred. The PRINCIPAL measures of statistical significance are as follows:

1. Chi square (X^2)

   When the obtained results take the form of frequencies, proportions, or percentages rather than scores, the most common index for measuring the statistical significance of differences in such ration is X^2. The value of X^2 at the 5% and 1% level varies with the number of categories or cells being compared and the number of cases in each cell. Accordingly, to evaluate a particular X2 value it is necessary to consult a table to be found in virtually every elementary statistical text.

2. Critical ratio (CR)

   This index is used to test the statistical difference between two means when the number of cases in each group is large. The critical ratio is nowadays being supplanted by the t-test (see below) which takes into account the number of cases in each comparison.

3. t-test

   This is the MOST common and MOST efficient measure of the statistical difference between two means. It is a ratio which again varies depending on sample size so that significant levels must be determined from appropriate tables appearing in elementary statistical texts.

4. F-test

   This is a more general case of the t-test, used for comparing not just two but any number of means. In the simple case where only two means are involved F equals t . The F-test is the basic index employed for analysis of variance (see below).

5. Analysis of Variance

   A type of experimental design that permits the testing of significant differences across several different dimensions at once. For example, in an investigation involving not only an experimental group and a control group but subjects of both sexes classified in four different socio-economic classes, it is possible through the use of a balanced design to apply analysis of variance to determine significant differences that may exist not only between the experimenta.1 and control groups, but also between sexes, and SES levels, as well as their various combinations. The analysis of variance makes use of F-tests to determine whether obtained results achieve required levels of confidence.

GLOSSARY OF STATISTICAL SYMBOLS

Σ: process of summation.

$\|$: the positive value of the quantity in between.

m: the value of an individual observation; the value of the mid-point of a class.

f: the number of observations (frequency) in a given class.

i: the width of the class interval, i.e., the difference between two consecutive class limits.

N: the total number of observations.

a: the value of an original observation (same as m); symbol a used in formula for the geometric mean; value of Y_c when $X = 0$ in equation of trend or in regression equation.

w: weight attached to a value entering into an average.

M: the arithmetic mean.

M': an assumed arithmetic mean.

c: the correction factor, the difference between an assumed mean and the actual mean ($M - M'$).

d: the deviation of a given observation from an average.

d': the deviation of the mid-point of a class from an assumed mean or arbitrary origin.

Md: the median.

Mo: the mode.

L_1: the lower limit of the modal class.

d_1: the difference between the frequency of the modal class and the frequency of the preceding class.

d_2: the difference between the frequency of the modal class and the frequency of the following class.

Mg: the geometric mean.

H: the harmonic mean.

Q_1: the first quartile.

Q_2: the second quartile; the median.

Q_3: the third quartile.

Q.D.:	the quartile deviation or semi-interquartile range.
K:	the value of a point which lies halfway between quartile one and quartile three.
A.D.:	the average or mean deviation.
σ:	the standard deviation.
V:	the coefficient of variation.
Coef. Q.D.:.	the coefficient of quartile deviation.
σ_M:	the standard error of the mean.
σ_s:	the standard deviation of the original observations in the sample.
σ_D:	the standard error of the differences between sample means.
σ_{md}:	the standard error of the median.
σ_{Q1}:	the standard error of quartile one.
σ_{Q3}:	the standard error of quartile three.
σ_σ:	the standard error of the standard deviation.
σ_p:	the standard error of a sample percentage.
p:	the proportion in the population expressed as a decimal; the probability of success in a single trial of an event.
q:	$1 - p$; the probability of failure in a single trial of an event.
T:	the critical ratio.
M_h:	a hypothetical statement of the mean.
sk:	the coefficient of skewness.
p_0:	the price of a single commodity or service in the base year.
p'_0:	the price of a second commodity or service in the base year.
p''_0:	the price of a third commodity or service in the base year.
p^n_0:	the price of the *n*th commodity or service in the base year.
p_1:	the price of a commodity in a given year.
p'_1, p''_1, p^n_1:	the prices of other commodities or services in the given year.
q_0:	the quantity, i.e., the barrels, gallons, bushels, and so forth, produced, consumed, bought, or sold, in the base year.
q'_0, q''_0, q^n_0:	the quantities of other commodities in the base year.
q_1:	the quantity of a commodity in the given year.

q'_1, q''_1, q^n_1: other quantities in the given year.

$\Sigma p_0 q_0$:   the summation of the products of the commodity prices times their quantity in the base year.

$\Sigma p_1 q_1$:   the summation of the products of prices times quantity in the given year.

$\dfrac{p_1}{p_0}$:   the ratio of prices in the given year to prices in the base year.

b: the "typical" change in the growth factor per X unit of time, or the "typical" change in Y for a given change in X, in functional analysis, least-squares straight line.

$\log a$:   the log of the value of Y_c for a trend or regression line where $X = 0$.

$\log b$:   the log of the "typical" rate of change in the growth factor per X unit of time, or the log of the "typical" rate of change in Y for a given change in X, functional analysis, least-squares geometric straight line.

r: the Pearsonian coefficient of correlation.

$\bar{r}$:   the coefficient of correlation adjusted for the number of observations.

ρ: the index of correlation (rho).

$\bar{\rho}$:   the index of correlation corrected for the number of observations.

σ_r: the standard error of r.

Sy: the standard error of estimate.

$\overline{Sy}$:   the standard error of estimate corrected for the number of observations.

k: the coefficient of alienation.

X: an observed value of a variable quantity.

x: value of a variable quantity expressed as a deviation from the arithmetic mean of values of X.

Y: an observed value of a variable quantity, the dependent variable in functional analysis.

Y_c: values of Y computed by use of formula for trend, or regression equation.

y: value of a variable quantity expressed as a deviation from the arithmetic mean of values of Y.

GREEK ALPHABET

Letters		Names		Letters		Names
A	α	Alpha		N	ν	Nu
B	β	Beta		Ξ	ξ	Xi
Γ	γ	Gamma		O	o	Omicron
Δ	δ	Delta		Π	π	Pi
E	ε	Epsilon		P	ρ	Rho
Z	ζ	Zeta		Σ	σ	Sigma
H	η	Eta		T	τ	Tau
Θ	θ	Theta		Υ	υ	Upsilon
I	ι	Iota		Φ	φ	Phi
K	κ	Kappa		X	χ	Chi
Λ	λ	Lambda		Ψ	ψ	Psi
M	μ	Mu		Ω	ω	Omega

———

CPSIA information can be obtained
at www.ICGtesting.com
Printed in the USA
BVHW010756110122
625978BV00011B/178